HAPPY
INDEPENDENCE
Day

4TH OF JULY

www.capitoltimesmedia.com

WELCOME TO CAPITOL TIMES MAGAZINE!

We are thrilled to have you join our readership, where we strive to deliver accurate and unbiased news straight from the heart of US Capitol politics to the broader global landscape. In an era dominated by sensationalism and misinformation, we stand firmly committed to providing you with the truth.

At Capitol Times, we understand the importance of staying informed about the political developments that shape our world. We believe that knowledge is power, and our dedicated team of journalists works tirelessly to bring you comprehensive coverage, insightful analysis, and in-depth features on the pressing issues of ourtime. From the corridors of power in Washington D.C. to the farthest corners of the globe, our magazine aims to present a holistic view of politics, ensuring that you have a well-rounded understanding of the forces shaping our collective future. We believe that it is through awareness and understanding that we can make informed decisions and actively participate in shaping a better society.

As you embark on this journey with us, we invite you to explore the diverse range of topics we cover. From domestic policies to international relations, from social justice to environmental concerns, we strive to provide a rich tapestry of information that reflects the complexity of our world. Our commitment to truth and integrity means that we are dedicated to upholding the highest journalistic standards.
We rigorously fact-check our articles and adhere to ethical reporting practices, aiming to present you with the most reliable and accurate information available. We understand that trust is the cornerstone of our relationship, and we value it above all else.

In addition to our news coverage, Capitol Times Magazine offers thought-provoking opinion pieces, engaging interviews, and profiles of influential figures in the political arena. We encourage you to actively engage with our content, to question, to challenge, and to share your own perspectives. Together, we can foster a vibrant community of informed citizens who are passionate about making a difference.

Thank you for choosing Capitol Times Magazine as your source for truth news. We are honored to have you on board, and we look forward to embarking on this journey of knowledge and enlightenment together. Welcome to the Capitol Times family!

Sincerely,

Capitol Times Magazine
www.capitoltimesmedia.com

CAPITOL TIMES MAGAZINE | ISSUE 1 | JULY 2023

CONTENTS

Capitol Times Media

THE INAUGURAL ISSUE
Volume one | July 2023

www.capitoltimesmedia.com

Editor-In-Chief
Anil Anwar

CONTRIBUTORS

Mary Jones | Andrew Joseph | Johnson Hall

Capitol Times Magazine

Published in the United States | All Rights Reserved 2023

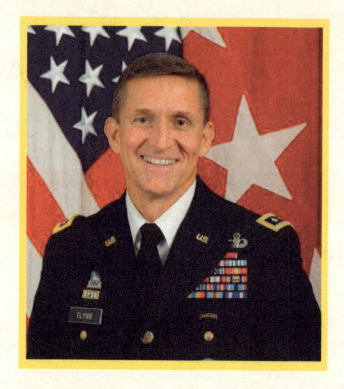

Statement by General Michael T Flynn

"Through my work as a senior intelligence officer in the world of national security and special operations, I have known about the courageous work Patrick Byrne has been directed to do on behalf of the United States Government. Most people don't understand the work of 'national intelligence assets' but that is what Patrick has been asked to be when it comes to the opaque world of government-to-government relationships. He's been placed into extremely difficult positions and has had to use his judgment to understand how to best accomplish his directed missions to the best of his ability.

This takes extraordinary judgment and courage. I've gotten to personally know Patrick over the past few years because of his USG directed role in rooting out corruption. He has been unshakable when it comes to his relentless pursuit of exposing the deep levels of corruption within our government. For a man who thought his life would be spent engaging an overseas adversary, he found himself battling his own government.

The incredible story of bribery, blackmail, rape, murder and other tales, normally the stuff found in fiction novels, are the truth coming from a man who was asked to enable, encourage or conduct these actions on behalf of our very own government. Patrick's story is for real, he's for real, the corruption he's exposed is for real, and it only gets worse the further you read."

THE EMERGENCE OF A CONTROVERSIAL MAN

"These days, when people talk of Byrne, the word 'vindication' comes up a lot," opened an article in the *Salt Lake Tribune* in August, 2008 as the financial system quaked into crisis.

Not long after, financial journalist Charles Gasparino scolded his CNBC cohosts on-air for how they had endlessly attacked Byrne regarding claims about which he had turned out to be correct: "Patrick Byrne was right, all along…the Overstock guy…that everybody made fun of…" rebuked Gasparino to a shame-faced Jim Cramer and Becky Quick.

Months later, Wall Street Journal included Byrne in its year-end list ("2008 Look back: Best Calls of the Year" [WSJ]of five people who deserved credit for seeing the financial crisis coming (others included Jamie Dimon, Nassim Taleb, and Nouriel Roubini).

On October, 2008 Alan Greenspan had explained to Congress the origins of the financial collapse, and gave testimony that became famous:

Dr. Alan Greenspan,
October 23, 2008

There are additional regulatory changes that this breakdown of the central pillar of competitive markets requires in order to return to stability, particularly in the areas of fraud, settlement, and securitization.

"By 'fraud,' Greenspan was referring to Bernie Madoff," says Byrne. "By 'securitization,' Greenspan was referring to the role played by Mortgage Backed Securities in the 2008 financial crisis. But when Greenspan said 'settlement,' he was pointing to what I had been saying to anyone who would listen. Metaphorically, since 2005 I had doused myself in gasoline and self-immolated in front of the SEC to warn the country about settlement failures and systemic risk, which Greenspan was telling Congress about that day in 2008. Everyone in financial circles knew that I had been proven correct."

It was a fitting denouement to one of the strangest sagas that ever played out on Wall Street. But it is as good a place as any to anchor the story of Patrick Byrne.

A   KURZIAN   FIGURE

According to PBS, Patrick Byrne is the "kingpin" of the movement that asserts that election integrity is significantly more sloppy than is generally understood, that election-rigging now occurs with methods beyond anything that can be discovered through rudimentary audits, and that the 2020 election was rigged. Byrne joined in calling for people to rally in DC on January 4-6, 2021. Though he insisted those rallies be peaceful, he has offered to pay the $350,000 of damages to the Capitol Building which gets tacked onto the charges of each J6 defendant, making their sentencing more severe. "I look at it this way," says Byrne. "Assume I invited a bunch of friends to a bar and somewhere in the evening a riot of suspicious origin broke out. As a gesture of goodwill, before we got to the subject of who really started the riot, my friends or the bar's doormen, I might be inclined to pay for the damages. Simply on the principle of, 'they were my guests, it got out of hand, I'll cover the broken mirrors and furniture... But now let us look at the security cameras and see who started the riot.'"

In addition, Byrne has publicly offered to face all non-violent charges from that day: those accused can say they did it because they listened to Byrne, and Byrne will agree to stipulate to this being the case, on the condition he can defend himself in televised proceedings. "I'll face the charges for 1,000 of the J6 rally-goers, right here in a DC court facing a DC jury. I won't face charges for anyone who broke a window or fought a cop, but I will for everyone who was peaceful, on the condition that I can defend my actions in a televised trial. Lay it on me and I will answer for it all to a DC jury."

Byrne delivers the idea with no hint of bluster or menace but in a friendly, helpful manner. In a similar tone, he notes that law enforcement from around the country who are receiving training at DHS have gotten word back to Byrneof a phenomenon he calls, "disconcerting." When traineers ask, "Whom do you fear more, Russia or China?" DHS trainers have been instructed to reply, "We are keeping our eyes on both, but above all we worry about this guy Patrick Byrne and the movement he has going."

According to Byrne, it started happening last summer, months before the 2022 election, and people who experienced it got in touch to let me know: DHS was telling people that I am Domestic Extremist Threat #1," says Byrne with a broad grin.

Over the years, Byrne's trajectory has reminded some of the character Colonel Kurz, from Apocalypse Now. A "golden boy" early in life, but one who ultimately goes off track through (according to some) insanity, genius, or some dark impulse that cannot be unraveled.

It is easy to find Byrne's manner and language disorienting at times. For this reason large sections of this interview will not be summarized, but will remain as Q&A transcript, for the reader to digest directly.

BYRNE'S CONNECTION TO WASHINGTON, DC

"I've had so many tailwinds it is almost comical," answers Byrne when asked about his life. "It is easy and not inappropriate to see it as a silver spoon. The truth is slightly more interesting: over my first 25 years my family lived a Horatio Alger dream, and I got to see it unfold." Asked to expand, Byrne answers obliquely, "For the 1960s the Byrne family was Tunafish Helper, for the 1970s it was Hamburger Helper, by the 1980s it was steak and lobster, by the 1990s it was King Airs, and from 2000 onward, private jets."

Only after some prodding does Byrne go into details, which reveal his connection to the DC area. According to him, "Both parents are from New Jersey Irish working-class backgrounds. My mother's father was a lineman in Cape May, New Jersey. My father's side was from Patterson tenements that were then Irish and Jewish, by the 1960's were Black and Hispanic, and are now Muslim. In the Depression they moved to Wildwood. Pop went Air Force ROTC to Rutgers, ticked off a General, served his years in an Ice Station in northern Greenland, discharged, married Mom. On the GI bill they moved to Michigan, broke-as-a-joke, so Pop could get a Master's in Math and land an insurance job, which had been his dream since he was 10, oddly. Michigan and Indiana are where we three kids popped into existence, I the youngest and smallest of three lads. Our dear middle brother passed away several years ago."

"While I was an infant we moved to New England. I grew up anchored to Vermont and New Hampshire as my father bounced among jobs in Massachusetts and Connecticut." Byrne tells an story about his youth. "Since childhood, our folks' message was, 'We will support you through you're education, but then you are on your own. Nothing can make us prouder than you focusing on education, but that is all you are owed.'"

Byrne launches into a story revealing his DC connection.

When Byrne was 13 his father was passed over for a promotion at an insurance company firm in Hartford. "When I was grown older, he let me know that he felt it was because he was Irish Catholic, in the mold of Tip O'Neil: big, garrulous, chubby. He also hired Jewish and Black people. How he saw it, the WASPs at HQ liked him because of his ability to work with insurance agents, who were often Jewish or Black, because they started one- or two-man insurance agencies to avoid the discrimination of big firms. But the brass did not like it at HQ, and were against a Catholic rising too far in the firm. The job went instead to a WASP guy out of Hollywood Central Casting, a man who never made his numbers, who over the next 20 years ran the company into the ground," says Byrne the younger. "I was with my father in his dying days and that setback still haunted him, though for decades I told him it was the best thing that ever happened to the Family Byrne."

Why that would be the best thing that ever happened to the Byrne family becomes clear as Byrne explains what happened thereafter. "Pop quit in disgust, and took a new job at a failing insurance company down here in the South, a job for which they could find no one else because the firm was going bankrupt. As a life insurance actuary he was an odd choice to run a car insurance company, but like I said, they could find no one else to take the job. So in 1976 we moved from New England to Maryland. He was at his new job only a week or two before he came home and said that he had a plan to save the firm. It would be... energetic." Weeks later, his father got a message that a Nebraska stockbroker wanted to meet and talk about what he was doing.

"My dad went down to see him and did not come home until dawn. Nothing like that had ever happened with my dad. When he came back in the morning he told us, "I just met the smartest man I've ever met in my life. He is some kind of farmer-stockbroker.'"

Byrne continued, "Our family had our order in for our first new car, a $7,000 station wagon. He had promised it to my mom to assuage her about the sudden move south. But he told my mom that morning we were canceling the new car and putting the money into the stock of his new friend. It turned out that his new friend was excited about the meeting, because he went out and bet 1/3 of his net worth on my dad." Finally Byrne drops his reveal. "That new job of my dad was at GEICO, which almost disappeared in 1976. And his new Best Friend Forever was Warren Buffett." Buffett was virtually unknown, and GEICO was 1/100th its current size.

According to Byrne, Buffett bet 1/3 of his net worth on Byrne's dad, and that became Buffett's first billion. "That $7,000 car, invested instead in Berkshire Hathaway stock in 1976, along with all the rest of the decade at GEICO, worked out ridiculously well for the Byrne family."

These years played out as Byrne attended high school at Bethesda's Walt Whitman High, '81 (a National Merit Scholar who went All-State in Football both ways, and county champion wrestler before taking up boxing at a DC gym called "Findley's Gym"). "I was the youngest and smallest of three boys," explains Byrne. "I grew up getting my ass kicked by my brothers. So while they learned to golf and kayak, as soon as I was able I wanted to learn to wrestle, box, and study whatever martial arts were handy."

During those years, Buffett would occasionally visit and stay with Byrne's family. "Mr. Buffett would call ahead and tell them, 'Have Patrick be home next Thursday at 11 AM for two hours.' In Dorothy Byrne's household there was no such thing as "'skipping school,'" but my parents were so enamored of this guy from Nebraska that they would pull me out of school just so I could sit with him for a few hours. Once I got a message from him, 'I'll be in New York City next week, come by such-and-such a hotel and spend Tuesday afternoon with me from 2-4.' One summer, I found myself hitchhiking around the county, and he had me stop in Omaha to take me to dinner at Gorat's, which has since become famous in Buffett- World."

Somewhere in those years, Byrne says, he and Buffett started to use the term "Rabbi" to describe Buffett's relationship to Byrne" (because it resembled the relationship a young Jewish boy would have with his own Rabbi). "It was absurdly generous of Mr. Buffett, looking back," says Byrne. "I was 13, maybe 14 when it started. I still remember verbatim parables Buffett told me. My life's direction was changed by those afternoon conversations he took for me."

Byrne describes his first foray into entrepreneurship. While a sophomore at Whitman High, he and his brothers created a Christmas Tree business run out of a parking lot off McArthur Boulevard, in Bethesda. Byrne can still recite the numbers: "500 trees bought for $8/tree in Maine and trucked down in a Ryder by my oldest brother that we were selling for $30/tree in Bethesda. So 500 trees X $22 gross profit equals $11k in gross profit, minus our expenses." Byrne and his brothers sold Christmas trees by a trashcan fire for four years, he says. "The first year we were making money on paper, but two days before Christmas 40% of our trees were unsold. That is when I first learned about 'overstock'. We took them to a Korean church in Virginia and gave it away two days before Christmas. But the second and third years, we netted about $8,000 with two weeks' work, and we three thought we had discovered the wheel. Then the fourth year someone else opened up in the same lot, and we learned why Buffett says, 'God loves a monopoly.'"

Byrne graduated from Whitman in 1981 then joined his two older brothers at Dartmouth College, in New Hampshire. Why did all three boys go to Dartmouth when his father had gone to Rutgers? "Growing up around northern New England, we always saw Dartmouth as the right place,when the time came. Frankly, we were by nature not Flatlanders. New Hampshire and Vermont were home, and maybe as a result, ever since, I have always conscious of being around city people. You know how to people in the city, folks from the country seem odd? It works the other way around, too. Frankly, if one comes from the country, then for the rest of your life, city people seem like *kooks*. What passes for normal behavior in city environments will, if you do it in the country, lead people to think you're an idiot. I had a great experience in at Bethesda's Walt Whitman High School, where a fantastic principle named Dr. Jerome Marcose led a wonderful institution. I had teachers and coaches with whom I stayed in touch for years out of gratitude for how they touched my life. I had wonderful friends through those years, whom I remember fondly.

But I could not wait to go back, and the day after I graduated I drove to a farm in Vermont, which became my favorite period in my life."

Byrne's family moved to Vermont and he soon began studies across the river at Dartmouth in Hanover, New Hampshire. There he majored in Philosophy (the Western kind, his favorite course being logic), and Asian Studies. He played football for two years and worked hard on the farm in off-seasons, he says. "I was a grind," says Byrne, "and decided that while at college I would never enter a party, a fraternity, or a church. I did not want to be in a room where everyone felt pressure to think the same way. I worked on the farm, and two or three days per week in class, and spent a lot of time in the library and language lab. Seasons went by where I spent days in the library and evenings studying Chinese." Giving up his last two years of college football, in 1983 Byrne went to China as it first opened to foreign students, spending a year at Beijing Teacher's University. Initially he studied Chinese language, but went on to Chinese history and philosophy. "It started with Laozi, Zhuangzi, Confucius, and a certain Tang Dynasty writer, but I continued through Marxist-Leninist-Maoist thought."

In 1983, seven years after the Cultural Revolution, Patrick Byrne was in Beijing studying Maoism? "Yep," replies Byrne cheerfully, and speaks what sounds like several sentences of Chinese (regarding Dialectical Materialism and the Cultural Revolution, he later explains).

From China Byrne went to Thailand for six months, studied Thai language and kickboxing, returned home to the USA to graduate after writing a thesis for each of his Dartmouth majors. One was a translation of Classical Chinese, the other, on Marx. "I was already trying to work out what was wrong," he tells me. "I had these wonderful teachers, both in China and in the US, who were Lefties. I suppose I was trying to make sense out of how that could be, how people so smart in so many ways were so backward in others. But I could not put my finger on it."

In that endeavor he was guided by a relationship with two philosophy professors visiting Dartmouth when Byrne returned. David Luban, now a Georgetown Law professor, and his wife, Judith Lichtenberg, of Georgetown Philosophy, both now distinguished philosophers. "David is known in many sub-disciplines, such a Legal Ethics, and is a famous figure in the Torture Debate," says Byrne. "Judy is a social and moral philosopher." Byrne says that both are well-regarded and associated with the Left.

"We have maintained an intellectual friendship for decades, one that generally has transcended our political differences. But now that DHS tells people I am Domestic Threat #1, things may be a bit chilly," Byrne says, sadly. "When they learn I was right about elections I fear they will never be able to forgive me."

THE CANCER YEARS

Up graduating Dartmouth, Byrne was diagnosed with cancer. It would hit him three times in his 20s, which he says were largely spent dealing with cancer and convalescing. He declines to discuss the subject further, but directs this magazine to what he says is the only time he ever discussed the subject.

https://www.pmc.org/blog/ pmc-threshold- moment-by- billy-starr

Byrne limits himself to dropping a few statistics about his health. Of roughly 22,000 nights on Earth, Byrne has spent over 800 in hospitals. He draws his collar aside and reveals a fresh surgical scar near the base of his neck, not even a week old, still bandaged. "Last week I had surgery #115: they removed a tumor. It was benign, humd'allah. I've had my heart stopped about 400 times. So I've ridden that Death Train about 500 times."

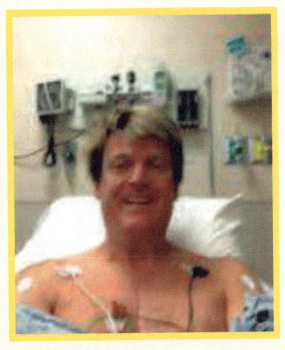

During his years in and out of hospital in his twenties, Byrne began graduate studies in mathematical logic at Stanford University, in Palo Alto, California. "Stanford Philosophy was tremendous to me, and those studies brought me close to a religious experience," says Byrne. "One hears about a botanist studying a flower and having a religious experience, seeing God in the petals of a rose. For me, it was that period of studying logic. One night I left Greene Library at midnight to ride home in the dark, and as I bicycled I had what I suppose was a 'religious experience.' For some it is the Bible, for some it is a rose, for me it was computation theory."

At Stanford Byrne first encountered what he now calls "Early Woke" and recognized it for what it was: "Maoism with American characteristics," Byrne says. Byrne explains what he says is the basic worldview of Marxists:

"'The world is divided into fools and knaves, and we need to protect the fools from being oppressed by the knaves.' That presupposes a third class of individuals, 'experts' who will make decisions for the fools and the knaves in order to keep minimize that oppression."

Byrne continues, "Let's move from pure Marxism to Maoism. Mao came to power in 1949 .But by the 1960s he was being put out to pasture, having made mistakes in his management of China, such as 'The Great Leap Forward'. So he called forth a "Cultural Revolution."

Byrne explains, "There were five bad categories of people (landlords, capitalists, rich peasants, right-wingers, and 'bad elements'), and five good categories (peasants, workers, etc.). Adults in bad categories were humiliated, trotted around town with dunce caps, tortured, rusticated, often killed. Worse yet, their children inherited their 'Bad'. The only way out of it for their children was to adopt a new identity: 'Red'."

"Map that paradigm to what is occurring here: 'Good' identities are 'intersectional', "Bad" is White, Cis, male, Christian. An alternate identity youth can adopt to redeem themselves is 'Woke' or some variant of 'Queer'. This is Maoist 'Movement Warfare' with American characteristics, *mutatis mutandis*."

Byrne won a Marshall Fellowship and went to Cambridge England for two years, switched from logic to moral philosophy, met legends of philosophy and economics, and also encountered Full Woke, "uninformed, anti-intellectual... Like current US university life."

Still convalescing in and out of hospitals, Byrne returned to Stanford and discovered that in just a few years it had started reorienting on a Woke agenda. He found himself reacting negatively against this "Woke" academic environment. "I found myself shifting to political philosophy, still trying to understand how people who were good and decent and smart in so many ways, could be so willing to jettison the values and principles underlying Constitutional republicanism for stale and uninformed Marxist bromides."

At Stanford he had studied the origin of such basic concepts as free speech, rights of the accused, and tolerance, but now found those principles being challenged and unraveling on the campus of a great American university. "I had always looked at World War II a bit differently than teachers wanted us to in school. Teachers wanted to tell us that the great lesson of WWII was, 'Don't be nationalistic.' That seemed incorrect. The real lesson from World War II was, 'When totalitarians challenge the values of political liberalism, stand up and defend them immediately. Don't surrender an inch.'"

Yet in the early 1990's he saw this happening in university "culture wars." Now he says that a glorious 2,500 year old intellectual tradition is at risk of being lost to what he calls "a horde of pseudo-intellectual European mediocrities" who turn out to have had no deep commitment to those principles and lack basic knowledge of history and economics, says Byrne.

ENTREPRENEURSHIP

During and after completing his PhD, Byrne worked in a variety of entrepreneurial endeavors. He was involved with liquidating real estate out of the S&L crisis, worked on Wall Street for a year, and developed a casino in Colorado. He led a variety of investment groups making tiny investments in business deals in northern New England and around the county.

"A Jiffy Lube in Florida needed to be bought out from TWA pilot getting a divorce; we'd buy it and tweak it a bit then refinance and get the capital into real estate in Manchester, New Hampshire. Then sell that project to get the capital into a printing company in Providence, Rhode Island. On and on."

Eventually Byrne ended up the majority owner/ CEO of a 20 person machine-shop telemarketing industrial parts from West Lebanon, New Hampshire for three years.

That is when Buffett called asked Byrne to come plug a gap for him for three months...that turned into two magical years. Byrne describes working for the man who had been his "Rabbi" since he was a teenager, but it is clear he feels uncomfortable revealing anything but scanty deals about their friendship. "I can talk about things he taught me," says Byrne. "That was our deal from the start. But I tend to avoid going into detail about our personal relationship."

By 1999 Byrne was considering settling down to the life of a professor, but started one last project: Overstock.com. With no venture capital or institutional backing Byrne turned Overstock profitable on tens of millions of dollars in capital compared to the hundreds of millions (or billions) used by competitors such as Amazon. He pioneered innovations in digital marketing and supply chains (such as "agile networked supply chains" and "B2C drop-shipping") that became part of the fabric of Ecommerce. Over 20 years his "one last project" emerged as a $2 billion giant, while Byrne earned accolades as "National Entrepreneur of the Year 2011" and Overstock as one of the "100 Most Trusted Businesses in America 2014" (of 8,000 public firms).

It was in the course of that career that Byrne got in his notorious fight with Wall Street. He says that as a public company CEO starting in 2002, he was meeting with various hedge fund players. Eventually, he said, he began to be taken to dinner and have muttered to him offers that began, "Hey kid, we could make a lotta money together… if you're willing to play ball." He reverse-engineered their schemes, then went to the authorities to explain what was going on around Wall Street. "Their inaction bordered on indolence," Byrne said.

By 2005, Byrne had started a battle over aspects of the Wall Street financial plumbing (the "settlement system") that, he said, allowed bad market participants to manipulate markets and destabilize the financial system. He claimed that the SEC was a "captured regulator" not truly policing Wall Street, but inappropriately close to Wall Street. It could pursue small fry but they were afraid to police the worst players on Wall Street either because those players had 'too much" (juice" (as one SEC senior was caught saying about the leader of a major Wall Street bank in 2008), or because they were thinking of their future employment and understood that lucrative offers only await those who "regulate" lightly.

In this battle, Byrne began to be helped by a swarm of people he met on Internet message boards, an army of activists cooperating to clean up Wall Street. It included researchers and investigators, stockbrokers, economists, lawyers, engineers, and writers who became an extended irregular force in support of the mission. "The *pajamahadeen,"* says Byrne. "That' is what I called them. It's like being a *mujahedeen*, but you get to do it at home from your Mommy's basement in your pajamas," he jokes.

"Milton Friedman famously said, 'There is no such thing as a free lunch.' As hedge funds and the finance industry uses such schemes to earn billions or trillions, those dollars are coming from somewhere. They are drained from people across America," said Byrne. "If one were walking down an alley and saw an old lady being mugged, one must get up in someone's grill. Unfortunately, I still thought the world worked like something out of *The Pelican Brief.* You know: Julia Roberts figures out the evil corporation's scheme, writes up her term paper, the DOJ and the *Washington Post* swoop in and investigate…" Byrne guffaws at the depths of his early innocence "No, what really happens is that forces of corruption emerge to distort, suppress, and bury the truth. Like what we are living through now."

Byrne explains that the Wall Street experience split into two parallel tracks. On the one track, he and his *pajamahadeen* were trying to figure out the various components of what Byrne calls, "Wall Street criminal mischief." Yet to Byrne, the second and more important track became: "How does Washington, DC react to the evidence we are surfacing? That became just as important a topic to unravel. I had data, I had Harvard PhD economists, I had Wall Street insiders, I had folks from the underbelly of it all. I knew that these settlement issues would lead to a crisis, and in the meantime, mom-and-pop investors were being ripped off. I went to see all the people one would think of seeing: the financial press, the SEC, FINRA, NASD, the House Financial Services Committee, the Senate Banking Committee. We discovered no matter what data and no matter what witnesses, they were all frozen. Finally, some staff started coming clean: 'Every time you are here, Byrne, you should know that Goldman and Morgan are in 10 times... and they are large supports of the Senator, you know...'"

Byrne tells about the day in 2006 that his assistant ran into his office, panicked: "The Department of Justice is on the phone!"

Byrne told her to put it through, and when he did, Caller ID confirmed it was the US DOJ. When Byrne answered, a male voice identified himself as Ken Breen, Assistant United States Attorney with the DOJ.

Byrne says he jumped to his feet and stood at attention, saying, "Yes Sir! How can I help you?" Byrne says now with a sigh, "It seemed natural. I held the DOJ in that high regard.'"

Breen started: "I want you to know that it is perfectly legal for me to be calling you. I gave my notice, today is my last day at the DOJ, I have packed my possessions from my office into a banker's box, and in five minutes I am walking out the door of the Department of Justice to start a new job. I wanted my last act at the DOJ to be calling you, and you to know there is nothing illegal about me doing so."

Byrne says he gulped. "Yes Sir. I understand."

Breen continued, "I want you to know that at the DOJ there are 30 or 40 people following everything you are doing... and cheering you on. You are doing the right thing. We were looking at ..." and then shared a bit about how their knowledge of the mischief had been evolving. He ended up saying they thought I was going down a blind alley regarding one thing I was talking about, but had I looked into this other area and considered such-and-such...? Then he started wrapping up his call."

Byrne says he was flabbergasted, and finally said, "Sir, thank you and please thank your colleagues. I just have to ask one thing: Why are *you* telling *me* this? You are a United States Attorney. Can't you folks...?"

"Breen cut me off," says Byrne, "saying words that will ring in my ear to my dying day. 'Oh Patrick, you have no idea how politicized the environment is within which prosecution decisions are made.'"

And said good-bye.

Byrne tells a story about the English Philosopher Bertrand Russell, who in the early 1920s was in India lecturing on the structure of the cosmos per Einstein's new General Theory of Relativity. In the middle of one of his university lectures, goes the story, a Hindu Cosmology professor stood up and said, "I'm sorry Professor Russell, you are incorrect. The universe rides on the back of a turtle."

Russell replied, "Oh really? Then what's the *turtle* ride on?"

"The back of another turtle," says the Hindu.

"OK, then what's *that* turtle ride on?" answered Bertrand Russell.

The Hindu replies, "I'm sorry Professor Russell, but it's turtles all the way down!"

Byrne laughs at the story, but then explains, "From 2005 forward we had everything one needed to understand what was going to happen in 2008, what Greenspan would later tell Congress in October 2008 was at the core of the financial crisis: settlement. All the data, the economists, the experts... For three years we took it all to the financial press, the SEC, the FINRA, NASD, House Financial, and Senatebanking.... And we found that it was just turtle all the way down."

yrne's accusations towards the SEC of "regulatory capture" were initially dismissed as "conspiracy theory." CNBC and the financial press tarred-and-feathered Byrne for two years.

In January 2007, Byrne says, he and his cousin (a man well-known to Wall Street) were invited to breakfast at the offices of Richard Chilton, one of the largest hedge funds, whose leader was what Byrne calls "a greybeard" of the industry.

Chilton opened the meeting saying calmly, "Patrick, I want you to know that you have become the most hated man I have ever known in my entire life. You used to be something of a Golden Boy on Wall Street, but now you could kill people and not be hated in this town like you are hated here now."

Byrne says he replied without hesitation, "Sir, I stand by everything I've done."

Now, as he tells the story, he adds with a conspiratorial whisper, "Ain't that high fucking praise? Please carve on my tombstone, 'Here lies The Most Hated Man on Wall Street 2007!" He chuckles. "And now you can add, '& Joe Biden's DHS Domestic Threat #1 !"

By 2007 there were some who began wondering if Byrne's criticisms of Wall Street were correct. News stories appeared raising that possibility, such as a Bloomberg special entitled, "Phantom Shares", which was nominated for an Emmy Award.

Then the financial crisis of 2008 exploded. Alan Greenspan was in Congress explaining that the crisis was found not just in fraud (Madoff) and securitization (Mortgage Backed Securities) but in Wall Street's "settlement system" that Byrne had been critiquing for three years. And the unhealthy relationship between the SEC and Wall Street was exposed to the general public until it went from a conspiracy theory to the stuff of late-night comedy.

As the 2008 crisis unfolded along precisely the lines Byrne had been predicting for three years, the press began writing things such as, "These days, when people talk of Byrne, the word 'vindication' comes up a lot…" And the Wall Street Journal named Byrne among the 5 who had seen it coming.

Byrne's political commitments have long run to what he calls "small 'l' libertarian and small 'r' republican." He says the formulation comes from Milton Friedman. At the end of Friedman's life, weeks before he died, Milton Friedman called Byrne, telling him that he and Rose knew the end was near and wanted to make a last change to the will. They had decided to ask Byrne to take over leadership of the Milton & Rose Friedman Foundation for 10 years after Friedman's death, before stepping away and changing the name.

Byrne says he was startled at the request but after a moment, agreed. But he added, "Sir, this surprises me. I know that on Wall Street I have gotten into it with a bunch of your admirers. I don't feel I have any choice about doing what I am doing, but I know that I have been acting like something of an Irish hothead…."

According to Byrne, Friedman thought about his answer for three seconds, "which was 2 seconds more than Milton ever needed to think of an answer to anything." Finally he replied, "You know something, Pat? Maybe what our side has been missing has been an Irish hothead."

Byrne says that to him, it was as though Isaac Newton had called and said, "Would you carry on in my name for 10 years after my death?" For 10 years Byrne led the Milton & Rose Friedman Foundation. After a decade he stepped down and changed the name to "The Foundation for Educational Choice." Located in Indianapolis, Indiana, it remains the intellectual center of gravity of the national movement for educational choice.

Byrne proudly shows us a page from the National Education Association website in 2008, where they list of its enemies. There, the massive union lists its well-known opponents: Wal-Mart and Starbucks are #2 and #3. There on the NEA website, they name enemy #1: Patrick Byrne. Says Byrne with a grin. "So I have been The Most Hated Man on Wall Street in 2007, the NEA's Public Enemy #1 in 2008, and Biden's DHS Domestic Extremist #1. My cup runneth over."

What are Byrne's political ambitions? Without hesitation Byrne replies, "Zero." Minutes later, Byrne is asked again, "Really: What are your political ambitions?"

"Zero. Sub-zero. Zero-degree-Kelvin-zero."

Byrne believes what the country is experiencing is due to corruption. "It is as Federalist #10 predicted," says Byrne. "In designing the Constitution, Madison wrote, they looked at previous attempts at Democracy, ancient and modern, looked at what made those experiments fail, and tried to design a better system. But they knew that there was a problem they had not figured out how to solve, the one that took down republics more than any other problem:: the problem of special interests and the corruption they bring. A short way to say 'special interests and the corruption they bring' is to say, 'capture'." Byrne looks pensive. "We have a lot of different problems, in one sense, but the common denominator of them is that our institutions have failed because of capture."

So in 2019, there Byrne was, CEO of a $2 billion Ecommerce company, National Entrepreneur of the Year, leader of one of the Most Trusted Companies in America, and heralded by *Wired Magazine* as "The Messiah of Bitcoin" for his early involvement in the field, and recipient of countless awards regarding his visionary leadership and entrepreneurship. Life was good.

https://www.wired.com/2014/02/rise-fall-rise-patrick-byrne/

Then, like Colonel Kurz, his methods became, "unsound." It was August 2019 when everything changed. Byrne says, "I was watching my country burn, and I knew the truth about a lot of things I had been involved in. As things boiled over I went to see my Rabbi, and in 20 minutes I explained to him the truth about what was going on. I had never seen him angry in my life until that moment, but he was angry. He paced for 20 seconds, and then said to me, 'Patrick, your country is burning. The analysis is this: The truth has to come out. Given that the truth has to come out, the sooner that it comes out the better. This cannot be another Grassy Knoll for 50 years.' He told me that I had an obligation to go public, regardless of the repercussions for myself."

Weeks later, Byrne resigned from Overstock and went on Fox News with Martha McCallum. He said that he had a relationship with the United States Government, that he had been present for the origins of the Russian Collusion Delusion and that the entire matter was a hoax. It had all been engineered, Byrne said, and claimed he had helped engineer it. He referred to involvement in another matter involving an investigation into the corruption of a federal official.

Then Byrne flew to Indonesia.

We are sitting with Patrick Byrne now. The Durham report has just come out. Byrne says that he knows more about the subject than any man in America. To prove it, he plays a short video of a retired US Attorney Brett Tolman from August 2019, explaining on Fox:

https://rumble.com/v2u1zek-us-attorney-acknowledges-patrick-byrne-on-bongino

"I know Patrick Byrne. I've known him for years. I spent 45 minutes on the phone with him today talking about it. When he indicates she has previously worked with the FBI and provided information, he's telling the truth. Back in 2005 and 2006, I was chief counsel for the Senate Judiciary Committee and he brought to us inside information about manipulation that was going on and Wall Street. It turned out that it was accurate, and it was investigated, and it became part of a much larger investigation. So my experience with him is very fascinating, because while he's eccentric, he has been accurate historically with me and with others."

Byrne plays that video then shows us a photo of Maria Butina, taken as they strolled through DC.

"Connect those two dots, what Brett Tolman said in that video and what this photo shows, and you arrive at an insight: I am the most qualified man in America to tell you the truth about the Russia Investigation," says Byrne. "I'll save the DOJ a lot of trouble and stipulate now: If I am lying about this to the public, I am committing sedition. There, that should make it easy to convict me. DOJ won't. Because it is true."

Byrne continues: "The Durham Report covers 50% of the truth, and exposes how intelligence was politicized, how RussiaGate was a hoax, and so on," says Byrne. "But it is also a cover-up of world-historic proportions. It is Volume II of the story, and they have hidden Volume I."

Byrne adds that he might have held his tongue and gone along with it, had he had confidence that the source of the corruption had been remedied. But he says he sees nothing of the sort, and that this means he must come forward with the rest of the story. In a series of events that have occurred around the country starring General Mike Flynn, the "ReAwaken America Tour," Byrne has dropped additional pieces of the story, a bewildering kaleidoscope of clues and stories that sound like Robert Ludlum meet Thomas Pynchon Now for the first time, Byrne's story is being told in print.

What is or was the nature of your connection to the United States Government?

I am not a spy; I have never worked with the CIA. But it has been one of the honors of my life that from time to time, on rare occasion, there have been other parts of the government who knew they could call on me to make a small contribution, generally a rather academic contribution, to some effort of theirs, often having to do with peace.

How did this start? Can you give any examples?

In 1983, I was a student in Beijing. I had a French girlfriend, another foreign student. By day I spoke Chinese, by night, French. One evening she and I were walking through a public place, and a small Asian man overheard us and came bounding up to us speaking French. It turned out he was from Laos, and was a General who had run a coup in his country years earlier, then been deposed. He was living in a state guesthouse in Beijing. He and I became friendly, and met for a few dinners. Eventually he asked me if he gave me a letter, could I deliver it to the US. I thought about it for a couple days, decided it seemed harmless enough, and did it."

My life for the next five years was intense. I stayed on 18 months in Asia, returned to the US, wrote two college theses, graduated, collapsed with cancer, spent a few years hospitalized and began graduate studies at Stanford. I was focused on mathematical logic, but enjoying excursions into other areas, including development economics.

One day at Stanford I got a message: the Chairman of the Joint Chiefs General Vessey knew about letter I had delivered in China five years earlier, and wanted to meet me. I went up to northern Minnesota and we spent a day together.

General Vessey was Ronald Reagan's two-term Chairman of the Joint Chiefs. As Vessey was retiring, Reagan asked that as his last service to the USA, he re-establish peaceful relations with Vietnam. General Vessey made a couple trips to Vietnam. His counterpart Foreign Minister Nguyen Co Thach had eventually told him, *If you Americans are serious, please do something humanitarian for us as a sign.*

General Vessey spent a day getting to know me, quizzing me, actually. Then he asked me to go to

Vietnam, where we had no diplomatic relations, but to whom I would be identified as having been sent by General Vessey. I would be hosted by the Vietnamese government. I was to come back with a report for the General as to how $250,000 - $300,000 could be spent doing the most humanitarian good for Vietnam.

Why me? I was not an Old Asian Hand, but I was indeed a *Young* Asian Hand. I spoke Chinese and French (and even pretty good Thai back then). I had a good knowledge of Indochina from the French conquest up through the Indochinese wars. I also was at Stanford studying Development Economics. And I had grown up as an entrepreneur in an entrepreneurial household.

I went to Hanoi and was hosted by the Foreign Ministry for two extraordinary weeks. I returned and wrote what was in essence a term paper with a dozen good ideas, all priced out with crude attempts at measuring human suffering reduction per dollar. For example, the Swedes had built a small plant that made artificial limbs, but years earlier it had run out of raw material: I calculated how many limbs could be produced from $100 of polyurethane and thus how many lives restored. I had found a dozen opportunities like that. I wrote them up in a term paper, estimating lives improved for every $100 in cost. My understanding is that they did all of my projects other than one (installing a large sound system throughout a Blind Person's Nail Factory in Haiphong: I went back in 1989 and did it myself).

It was simple, back-of-the-napkin type of stuff. I was perplexed as to how such work could possibly be of service to the United States Government. With the benefit of decades of hindsight, of course, I understand better. To take a conventional approach to a nation with whom the USA had been at war and with which it had no diplomatic relations, and sending to it a fact-finding mission to conduct the same analysis.... [Byrne laughs]. Now I know enough to understand why General Vessey did what he did. The conventional approach would have included months of oversight, government lawyers signing off on things, millions of dollars. Instead, he found a grad student with relevant knowledge whom he could send over, spend a couple weeks, and be back with his term paper in hand, all inside of a month and for about $5,000 in expense.

Importantly, in 1988 I was identified to the Vietnamese government as doing this favor for the USA. As they were a Soviet client state, one must assume that the Soviets, and hence the Soviet KGB, knew of it as well. That means that in 1988 the Soviet KGB knew I was doing a humanitarian favor for the USG. Thus, in case you are wondering: I have never had anything to do with our Intelligence Community. When one is identified to the Soviet KGB in 1988 as doing something like that for Uncle Sam, it makes that it impossible to work for the CIA. I had never expected to, but since that is the first place people's minds go I thought it best to clear it up.

Anyway, I don't claim any great credit, I did nothing but make the tiny contribution I described. But it greased the next step, and the next... anyway, it took years of back-and-forth between Foreign Minister Nguyen Co Thach and General Vessey, but by 1994 peaceful relations were restored.

General Vessey passed away eight years ago but he had a protégé, General William Nash, who might be able to confirm that story.

So what was next?

I'm not excited about going into it much. It has been the honor of my life that on rare occasion, I had an opportunity to field a request from someone in some part of the US government, so it feels dishonorable speaking of it publicly, and I assumed word of it would never reach the world until after my death, if ever. But these are odd times, and I have no choice.

One thing I should make clear is that my contribution has primarily been academic: they invite me to come to a government facility and share my thoughts on a subject, usually one I have been writing and speaking about publicly. I get a month's notice, I show up and deliver a PowerPoint with my thoughts, and then I am escorted out and that is the last I hear of it.

Here is a good public example of the kind of talk it has been my occasional honor to present in government circles. Some years ago I spoke on "Economic Warfare as an Instrument of Transnational Organized Crime" to the Institute for World Politics in Washington DC. That talk is based on a talk I gave in government settings on other occasions.

https://www.youtube.com/watch?v=6FiAHVxCrbQ

So if you want to know what I mean by saying that the core of my relationship has been academic, and I am invited to give PowerPoint's, watch that link and you will get a good idea. Evidently my name is in some database as a "Designated Expert," though an expert in what, Iam not precisely sure.

But it also means that on rare, rare occasion, I might get contacted and be asked to do something like what I just described about Vietnam in 1988. Generally it has to do with an opportunity for peace.

One time a couple decades ago I asked an NSC official making a request of me, "Are you guys that hard up? Why do you folks ask me to do these things?"

The NSC official said, "Patrick, sometimes in this world, before certain kinds of people talk, other kinds of people need to talk. You are... that *other* kind of person."

Because it has been such an honor, talking about it feels disloyal. I am sorry to have had to reveal what I have told you. But given where our country is today, I think I do not have any alternative to share what I am going to share.

Three additional points become relevant. One concerns security clearances, one concerns Iran, one concerns Venezuela.

First, because of this side-gig of mine, a security clearance was kept for me for many years so I could receive briefings. That becomes relevant when we discuss the Russian Collusion Delusion.

The second is that around 20 years ago, whenever I was in Asia there seemed to be people from Iran making a point to find reasons to bump me and invite me to come to Iran. In 2006 I was directed (if I was willing) to accept one of these invitations and see who was behind them. I got a very open-ended tasking simply to go to Iran, socialize, and see where I ended up.

I went to Beirut and gave a talk at a university there regarding corruption and development. Some Iranians were in the audience, and afterward they made a point to befriend me. They invited me to Tehran. I went, schmoozed and swanked and schlemiel-ed around for two weeks, gave a talk on John Rawls, and came back Best Friends Forever with General Qasem Suleimani, and the Quds Forces were my boys.

For a decade I have heard that the Iranians tell people there would have been war between Iran and the USA in 2006 were it not for the events set in motion by that visit. I do not know what that was because after I came back other people took over.

In addition, and again, I am only sharing this because it becomes relevant when I left Overstock in 2019 I went SCUBA diving in Indonesia. General Suleimani sent word that a big war was coming and Iran wanted to tell the USG they wanted me to act as an interlocutor, as the American they trusted. I let him know I was deeply hesitant to get involved as I was then on-the-run from the USA, but I sent word to USG.

This was autumn 2019 and given everything else going on, the answer I got was... what I could only describe as confused and indecisive. In addition, it was getting increasingly difficult for me not only to surf, but even to walk due to what would prove a tumor on my spinal cord, so I declined General Suleimani's offer. Two months later the USA iced Suleimani.

I do regret that I did not give that one more of the old college try. As a World War II veteran, General Vessey used to teach me, "Any world where Russia, China and the US get along is better than any world in which we three do not get along."

I know from personal experience that the war going on today is the most avoidable war of our lifetime. It was so avoidable, it makes me suspicious it was manufactured for other reasons, quite possibly, out of domestic political considerations.

I wish I had sucked it up and made the trip.

The third story I will mention (and again, I mention these stories now only because they become relevant later) is that back in 2018 I was in Venezuela. There was something upon which Venezuela and the USG could have cooperated to the benefit of both, and I was there to find out if it was possible. The enmity proved such that it turned out to be impossible. But I had an interesting time in Venezuela.

I only mention this one because more recently, regarding Election 2020, I made claims regarding Venezuela and their computer science capabilities. From that herd of independent minds that is modern American journalism, the response was, *Byrne, what the hell do you think you know about Venezuelan computer science capabilities?*

Here is a photo from the official Instagram account of Venezuela, March 6, 2018. That is I, standing in a government computer science center in Caracas, Venezuela.

Let that stand for my response to 90% of the criticism I receive. Tedious journalists run their mouths without any idea what they are talking about and no awareness of how pseudo-intellectual they are. I think back to university, and remember that the students wanting to go into journalism were invariably the second dumbest students in any course I ever took or taught (the dumbest students being the football players, which I can say because I was one).

OK then. Fast forward to 2015. How did you get tangled up in current events?

Have you seen the clip of Maria Butina asking Candidate Donald Trump a question, in a conference in Las Vegas in July 2015?

Yes

That was 2015 FreedomFest, a summer libertarian conference that occurs in Las Vegas, Nevada.

Here is the schedule of that conference from 2015. You will see that Donald Trump was the Closing Day Keynote. Also, that three days before Trump spoke, I was the Opening Day Keynote.

https://freedomfest2015.sched.com/grid/

After I spoke, Maria approached me (she had landed in Vegas that morning). She identified herself as the leader of a Russian group resembling our NRA. What she did not know was that of 2,000 people in the room that day, I was the least interested in guns. I have a few, I keep proficient, but I see them as tools, not something to fetishize. So I brushed Maria off.

Maria came up the next day, told me she had a message for me from Russia, and asked if I would take a 90 minute meeting. I did. In it, I learned that Maria was, first of all, an extremely impressive young woman. She had a degree in political science, with had superb knowledge of literature and history, both Russian and American, and knew our Constitution's intellectual history better than most Americans, by a long shot.

Maria was known across the Russian power structure, to both Kremlin and oligarchy. I could share many examples, but the best would be her relationship to General Mikhail Kalashnikov, whom to Russians is something of a mythical figure. Kalashnikov was a WWII soldier who went to work in an arms factory, where he designed and built a weapon that in 1947 was released: the AK-47. In Russian worldview, it's "The Gun That Freed the World". At age 93, Kalashnikov had started an organization and named 23- year- old Maria Butina to be its president. The fact that 93-year- old General Mikhail Kalashnikov had selected 23 year old Maria Butina to be the leader of his organization meant something to me. Maybe that's because of my relationship with Milton Friedman, of which Maria was aware, or Vessey, of which she was not.

Maria told me she had been sent to America to do what she called "citizen diplomacy," hoping to be a force for peace, she said. She was going to be living with a Republican boyfriend in DC and going to graduate school, but she and Torshin (her "mentor," she said) had decided she should focus on building relations into the Hillary, Cruz, Rubio, and Trump camps, so that whoever won the election the following year, the Russians would have a back-channel relationship into the administration.

Maria invited me to fly to Moscow and give a talk on Bitcoin to the Russian Central Bank, then head to a private meeting for three days in a resort in the Altai with 45 people from across the Russian power structure. I don't want to pretend that stuff happens to me every day, but in the context of my life, it is not as strange as it may sound. In fact, it was happening a lot to me in those days.

As the holder of a security clearance I had an obligation to report her invitation to Russia before going, and likely an obligation to report such a conversation as well. In addition, I was 60% optimistic that this could lead somewhere good: as I have indicated, I had played a tiny role in a handful of peace events, and stranger things have happened. But I was also 30% concerned that there was a Russian woman who planned on swanking around our DC political class, and who had contacts across the Kremlin and oligarchy, including Russian FSB (she had told me

that when I went to Moscow they would question me, and counseled me to be direct and honest, but not elaborative, and that everything would be worked out by the people inviting me). There was an additional 10% reason, but only later will I explain that.

That evening my report of our meeting had reached Washington, DC. Later I was informed that it was a red flare over Washington, that it reached all necessary players that evening.

The significance of that is as follows: When in that famous clip from Las Vegas, Maria Butina stood up and asked Candidate Donald Trump a question, the federals already knew about Maria. Two days earlier they had received word from me, and my report had shot around Washington. I promise, when Maria asked that question, there were federals all over her. July 2015, not 2016.

So that's why you say that Durham skipped the first year of the Russian story.

Yes.

OK, what happened next?

What happened next is that Uncle Sam began acting out-of-character. Although I was not active with that kind of federal at that time, a message from me such as that would normally receive curiosity. Instead, for two months I only received replies along the lines: *We are not sure if there is anything to this, we are not sure if you should see Maria again or go to Russia, up to you, maybe you should, we don't really know.*

I promise, in such circumstances, Uncle Sam is normally not wishy-washy. I finally let them know: "I am not seeing Maria again unless you folks use the word 'greenlight' with me."

I got back a simple message: "Greenlight"

So you saw Maria again.

Yes.

And it turned romantic.

Yes.

How quickly?

Once I saw her again? Five seconds. Maybe three.

Let me mention that Maria Butina is something of a super-human. In Russian they test every 6 year old for mental and physical superiority, and select the top 30 to go to some special school: it's a holdover from the Soviet era. When Maria was 6 she was selected for that school, attended for a decade, graduated #2. At the time I met her, Maria was the Greater Moscow Women's Powerlifting Champion. She'd also get on a treadmill, run for 60 minutes at speed,with perfect form throughout, like the Terminator.

She is also a brainiac. If you want to know how smart Maria is, download an app called "Lumosity" and get the paid (harder) version. Our love notes back- and-forth were our daily scores: once she had used it a few times, every day she scored >99% among the millions of people who use it. My point being: Maria could take care of Maria, don't worry.

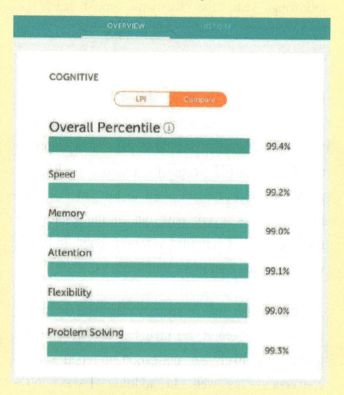

So how did the relationship develop?

At the end of the weekend I suggested to Maria that any time she was bored of her Republican boyfriend she should give me a call, we would pick a city she wanted to see, and meet for a 3-4 day tryst there. I give great tryst. I have no Act III whatsoever, but I have a great Act I and Act II. So I told her we'd meet for occasional trysts. I wanted to see her again, naturally. But that would

But it would also give me a great way to keep tabs on her, and to get to know her in preparation for perhaps opening doors she wanted opened. Not into the political class, but to the thinker-bees... And lastly, for reasons that you will soon understand, I wanted to see what they would do with Maria.

So you two began having an affair, while she was reporting to the Russian government, while you were to the US government?

Yes. I know it may seem odd. In the context of my life, which Uncle Sam knows down to every tick- and-jottle, none of this is strange. But I grant it may seem strange.

Do you realize it may sound not "strange" but "sinister" to some people?

Yes. Withhold judgment. I had ulterior motives you do not understand yet.

By November 2015 I knew what they were doing. Maria had met with and checked off someone in Hillary's circle (and, it turned out later, the federals then gave a prophylactic briefing to Hillary to keep Maria away). But she was still pursuing Cruz, Rubio, and Trump. The feds were letting it happen. They knew of virtually all of Maria's meetings, often *before* they happened, from me.

For example, Candidate Chris Chrystie sent word that he was going to be in New Hampshire and wanted to meet me. I was instructed to bring Maria and bring her to the meeting with Chrystie. "When she reports it to Moscow it will make your stock go up," the federals said. So I picked her up in a helicopter from New York and whisked her to New Hampshire. I met with Christie for an hour, and brought Maria in for the last 5 minutes. I later was told that they used that to get a warrant on Chrystie. Anyone who met Maria more than glancingly, they could get a FISA warrant on, along with anyone *they* know. Two hops.

In another case, Maria's pillow talk was that some powerful Republicans were trying to arrange a meeting between her and Don Jr. There would be a convention in the South (either about guns or a Christian conference). On Sunday at 2:30 PM Don was to be taken down the back elevator of his hotel and snuck out the back into a car that would take him across town to Maria's hotel, where they would meet for one hour.

I asked the FBI, "What do you want me to do? Whisk her off to the Bahamas for the weekend? How you want me to disrupt this?"

To my amazement they said, "Let it play."

That is what you mean when you say that the government, "started acting out of character"?

Precisely. There is *no way* the FBI would normally let that happen. They would warn the target. Incidentally, in the end, her private meeting with Don Jr. did not happen, though both Maria and Don Jr. attended a small dinner with a dozen or two dozen people.

By November, 2015 I knew we were manufacturing a scandal on the Republican Party. I mentally called it, "Can-O- Russia-Scandal". It was going to sit on the shelf until they needed it, and when they needed it, they would take it off, shake it up, crack it open, and spray scandal all over the Republican Party. I thought they were acting funny in July, August, and September 2015. By November 2015, Thanksgiving, I knew that is what we were doing.

That is when they came to me and said, "We have something more important for you to work on. FBI needs your help setting up Hillary Clinton for a bribe."

This conversation occurred around Thanksgiving, 2015, in a room with two federal agents. I maintain this is essentially word-for-word what was said to me:

Patrick, there are two groups in the FBI investigating Hillary Clinton. There is one group looking into Hillary's emails, but we all know that's a whitewash. But a group of agents in New York City are looking into her finances, and they want to put her away.

They walked me through the principles distinguishing a good sting from entrapment:

*An undercover cop can't just walk down the street, go up to a stranger, and say, "Hey, do you want to buy some cocaine?" That would be **entrapment**: the target would have been drawn into a **trap** of committing a crime that he probably otherwise would not have committed.*

*We can't have police running around creating crimes that would not otherwise happen, Patrick. So instead, a prosecutor needs to be able to show that the accused already had a **prior disposition** to buy*

*the cocaine, which is done by proving that the person had already performed one or more **predicate acts**, such as, "He pulled his car over at a street corner known for drug distribution, he put his car in park, he rolled down his window..." These **predicate acts** demonstrate that the accused already had a **prior disposition** to buy the cocaine, and so when the undercover cop approached and sold it to him it was not **entrapment**, but a crime that was going to happen anyway. So it is a good bust.*

Comey had been blocking "aggressive investigative techniques" (i.e., a sting) on Hillary, they told me, claiming there were insufficient predicate acts to establish that she had a prior disposition to accept a bribe.

We all caught eyes as he said that, because we all read the newspaper and it seemed hard to believe, but I said nothing.

The agent continued: Recently information had come in that Hillary accepted a $20 million bribe from a foreign government. They told me the government that did it and how it was done. The New York FBI agents had leveraged that information as the **predicate act** to force Comey to sign off on setting Hillary up in a bribery-sting.

Those New York agents were asking for my help. It was believed that Azerbaijan (a country to which I had never previously traveled) wanted to bribe Hillary in return for having Hillary pledge what one aspect of what her stance towards Azerbaijan would be. My assignment:

Patrick, you are going to create the following end-state: Somewhere in the world there is going to be a room. Hillary Clinton is going to go into that room, and the bagman is going to step into that room. They are going to spend 10 minutes alone together in that room. Then they are going to leave separately. You have two months to make that happen anyway you want, Patrick.

I told them that I thought it was dicey. USG and I always did business on a hand-shake (I had always said, "the fewer pieces of paper between us the better"). But now they were asking me to get involved in a federal election and bribe a presidential candidate.

I told them that it was that rare request for which I would need one of their "Acts Otherwise Illegal" letters (which are letters they can give you if, as the name suggests, you are asked to do something that would otherwise be illegal).

They said they would go discuss it with their bosses. A few days later we met again. One agent said: "We've been instructed to inform you that you cannot be *given* a letter, but if you'll come to DC, the Director says you can be *shown* a letter…"

I said, "This is coming from Director Comey?" Both Special Agents began nodding- coughing into their fists as they glanced and pointed up to the ceiling, while still coughing into their fists. I asked, "The Director and…. the President?"

They held my eyes as they coughed into their hands and nodded, together.

"OK, well, you can tell Director Comey and President Obama that" (I coughed into my hand as they had) "from them is good enough for me. Consider Hillary bribed."

Just like that? You agreed?

Yes. And seven weeks later, on the morning of January 14, 2016, Hillary met the bagman in a hotel room in DC. It worked like this: Hillary was on, say, the 8th floor of the hotel, her assistant was on the 5th, and she had a limousine at 9 a.m.

At 8:30 the bagman came to the hotel and went up to the assistant's room. At 8:47 Hillary left her room and took the elevator down as though she were going to the ground floor. But she popped off at 5 and went to her assistant's room. The assistant stepped out and waited outside the door. Hillary and the bagman spent 10 minutes together alone, then she came out, went down the elevator, and left in her limo by 9:02. It does not show up in her schedule but that is how it was done. January 14, 2016.

A few days later I met with the agents. I thought it might be the first time they showed personality. They had always been super-professional with me; never a trace of political inclination had been disclosed. They knew I am "libertarian republican" but I never showed political favor. I really tried to hold myself to the same ethic that military officers and federal officers do, about separating my political thoughts from my job. Or my avocation, in this case.

Still, I thought it might be a time that they'd surprise me. I didn't expect them to have a bottle of champagne, but I thought they would be happy.

Instead, the agents were more stern than I had ever seen them. They never mentioned whether or not Hillary had taken the bribe. Instead, they said, "Patrick, this mission has been re-analyzed, and it's been scrubbed. We need you to forget every moment of it. We mean it. You must erase every second of this from your memory."

They gave me this explanation with (feigned?) nervous and panicky tones:

This was all looked at again. Hillary Clinton is going to be our next president and nothing can stop that now. The day she becomes President, the first thing she is going to do is send her people over to the FBI and find out who was part of investigating her, and we are all going to be destroyed. That includes us and our own chain-of-command. It includes you too, Patrick. So this mission has been scrubbed from the highest levels.

They sat back and gauged my reaction. I agreed to forget it. But when I want home, it did not sit well with me. They could have performed their analysis before they tasked me. They seemed to be feigning their sense of panic. And, odd as it may sound, it did not seem fair to the Democrats: we had spent the 90s with a Democrat in the White House under perpetual investigation, and it seemed like the right thing to do was let them pick a clean candidate, not repeat the 90s.

In early February 2016, I met with the two FBI agents again. They brought a third, for the following reason. They said that in 2008 a law was passed that made it possible for the Director of Central Intelligence to sign a piece of paper, under certain circumstances, and take over the FBI. Director Brennan had done that on matters relating to Russia. So the DCI would be driving the FBI. They did not say exactly when Brennan had signed that, but they may have indicated it was some months earlier.

I previously said that I had never had anything to do with the CIA because I had been identified to the Soviet KGB in 2008 as doing a humanitarian favor for the USG in Vietnam in 1988. But I understated it: I had a red line, and that is, I would never work for the CIA. I was interested in tasks involving peace, and that was inconsistent with snooping for them. So it was always part of my understanding with USG that nothing I was involved in had CIA involvement.

But here was an odd situation: The CIA was not involved, they were nowhere to be seen. In fact, I sensed it was all being kept *away* from the CIA, deliberately. But the *Director* of the CIA was now giving orders to the FBI, which had just had me set up a Russian Collusion "Can-O-Russia-Scandal," and had just had me bribe Hillary Clinton then tell me to forget it ever happened. And now John Brennan's FBI go-between was sitting with us.

I let them know that their explanation as to why I needed to forget it did not sit well with me. And after some hemming and hawing, this is what I was finally told that first week of February, 2016, from three federal agents:

What's going on, Patrick, is that at this point President Obama has his people across the federal bureaucracy, but especially the Department of Justice. Hillary is going to be president for eight years and nothing is going to stop that. But while she's president, think of there as being a "Bunsen burner" inside the DOJ, and the evidence about the two bribes you know about is going to be sitting on that Bunsen Burner. The

hand on that Bunsen burner is going to be of one of Barack Obama's people. If Hillary is a good girl, defends Obamacare and such, that flame will stay on "Low". If she is a bad girl, if she starts thinking for herself, that hand [mimes twisting a dial] will turn the Bunsen burner to "High". That way, for the eight years she is President, Hillary is going to be managed by Barack Obama. Then Hillary is going to step down, and Michelle is going to run ...And Patrick, that's the plan.

Later I learned that the name of the plan was, "Operation Snow Globe". Hillary was to spend eight years as president in a Snow Globe that Brennan, Comey, and Obama could shake up anytime they wanted.

I have never disclosed this before, but one additional thing was said. One of the federal agents leaned in and quietly added, "So you see what we are saying, Patrick, is that when we tell you that you have to scrub every second of this from that memory of yours, it's really ... a matter of life and death."

Except he did not say "life and death": instead he said, "it's really ... a matter of life-n-d..." then nodded his head on the last beats completing the sentence. I nodded them along with him. We locked eyes and he raised an eyebrow the tiniest amount to see if I got it, and I gave him an almost imperceptible nod to match. He leaned back, satisfied but sad. The two other federal agents stared at their shoes. I wish to be clear that none of the agents thought this was copacetic. Their delivery was not proud or threatening, not "That's just the way it's going to be, Motherfucker." Just the opposite. Behind their gruff MIB-exteriors they were ashamed, and they spoke in a matter-of-fact and measured fashion, with pauses for me to catch up, but with an air of sad finality, as if to say, *it would help if you just accept this, because we're all in the deep end together*. They were family men, and my strong suspicion is that their lives and families were being threatened as well. They looked like they dreaded delivering me that message.

Now in case you are wondering: You may *think* you've lived, I thought *I* had lived… but you've never lived until you've had the personal liaison between FBI and CIA Director John Brennan sit in a room telling you that you just took part in a soft-coup, Obama versus Hillary, Obama is going to be president for 24 years, and if you open your mouth you are going to be killed. All while two other FBI agents who know you well sit on either side of him looking at their shoes either in horror, or because (unlike Brennan) they knew me well enough to suspect it was going to be a mistake. Or both.

I immediately flashed to late summer, 2006, when some Senate Institutionalists asked me for a favor.

Byrne is walking along the C&O Canal, on a path he says he used to run in high school. He has been talking of coaches and teachers, his upbringing, his life. He warns that what he is about to explain will sound odd. When informed he already crossed that Rubicon, he laughs and promises that, no, it is only now that the story gets truly odd, in two more installments.

Byrne reminds this magazine that when he told us of his fight with Wall Street 2005-2008, he had described Washington, DC as "turtles all the way down," his metaphor for a stack of compromised institutions. Now he informs us that he left out something big: the Senate Judiciary Committee. They found him, he says, came to understand that he was correct, and put him to work. Byrne explains how it happened.

According to Byrne, in 2005 Senator Orrin Hatch called to invite Byrne for a walk. Overstock.com was located in Salt Lake City, Utah, and Hatch was on a visit to his home state. "We had met in the past," says Byrne, "and he had visited our company once. It was a unusual, but of course I switched my schedule for him."

At some point in their walk, Byrne says, Hatch told him that he had come to learn that Byrne had an unusual relationship with the United States government. He asked Byrne to confirm it. "I told him I did not know what he was talking about. Which led to an invitation to a second walk."

"On the next walk, Hatch again confronted me about his understanding that I had had some kind of unusual relationship with the US government, and this time cited some specifics. I would have just kept on lying, but this was an imposing Senator, who reminded me of his seniority on various oversight committees of government. Eventually, I acknowledged he was correct."

"Hatch immediately turned on his heel, continued the walk, and it was a settled matter between us." Byrne adds with a chuckle. "Hatch was a shrewd man. He played that perfectly. Looking back, he was chopping off an avenue of retreat for me, a chance for me to equivocate. Then as we walked, he said one specific thing, which I remember because Arlen Specter repeated it when we met."

What did he say?

He said, "Patrick, they say you are a fellow who does... extreme things... to accomplish *whatever* he is asked to accomplish."

Why had he heard that about you?

[Byrne reflects before answering.]

There were a handful of times I had been asked to accomplish things they told me they did not have a method to accomplish themselves, given their rules, but they would turn a blind eye if I would do it for them. I would go and do it. They'd be happy until they found out how I did it, and then they would lose their shit. "You did what? What?!?! Do you have any idea how many rules you broke?" That happened occasionally. I suppose Senator Hatch may have heard about that.

In any case, Hatch asked me to meet with staffers from the Senate Judiciary Committee, to present the same evidence that I had been bringing to that stack of "'turtles all the way down,'" which is to say, the rest of DC. Evidence that the Wall Street settlement system had cracks in it, bad guys had figured out how to game the cracks to make money, it was harming investors, firms, corporate voting, and would destabilize the financial system (just as three years later, Greenspan would testify to Congress in the heart of the 2008 financial crisis). But we had figured it out in early 2005, and had been bringing the data, economists, and whistle-blowers to the SEC, FINRA, NASD, Senate Banking, House Financial Services... They would listen politely, or maybe impolitely, then shut the door with no response.

So Hatch had me bring to the Judiciary Committee those same data, economists, and whistle-blowers that we had brought elsewhere to no avail. After about 2-3 meetings, the Judiciary folks were like, "'Yep, you're right. Clearly that's illegal and harms the market. Now let's talk about who you have been bringing this information to, and what their responses have been.'"

Eventually they explained to me, "The Senate Judiciary Committee is the ultimate protector of the Constitution. That is because we investigate corruption. Our mandate to investigate corruption *transcends* every other power within government. If we suspect there is corruption in the manufacture of nuclear weapons, for example, we look into it and nobody gets to tell the Judiciary Committee that we don't have proper clearances. Our powers transcend everything in government because we investigate corruption, Patrick. And 'corruption' is anything that 'can be touched by a civil or criminal penalty.' Which is every aspect of life. Which means, Patrick, the Judiciary Committee investigates anything in the United States it wants to investigate."

So a small number of colleagues and lawyers who worked with me began interacting with them on these issues. They had us meeting with various officials in the SEC, DOJ, and regulatory bodies, and then reporting back to them about those officials. Frankly, they had us do that within Congress itself.

Soon I was told to bring two insiders to meet Senate Judiciary Committee Chairman Arlen Specter. What I knew of Chairman Specter was that he had been a Democrat federal prosecutor in Pennsylvania, was elected to the House as a Democrat, then to the Senate, but along the way he transitioned to being a Republican. However, before we met I was told he was de-transitioning back to Democrat, though I don't remember if that was public yet.

I brought two deep-inside Wall Street insiders from Staten Island. Chairman Spector spent 15-20 minutes listening to them, indicated he understood what what they had told him, believed it, and turned to talk to me.

Chairman Specter was going through cancer treatments. His hair was wispy from chemotherapy, and he had a gauze pad on the right side of his throat with access to a vein, much as I had lived with for years. We spoke of cancer, and then my ife.

It was an unexpectedly strange conversation. I thought we would be talking about things like Wall Street's Option Market Maker Exemption. Instead, he had me walk through my background, my upbringing, and even asked if I had had a religious upbringing. I told him that I tended to describe my teenage years as, "I majored in Catholic and minored in Jew." He was Jewish, and thought that was funny.

Bizarrely, Specter asked if I had been an altar boy, and I told him that I had. I happen to remember that distinctly, because in 30 years I don't think it had come up in conversation or, frankly, even crossed my mind. In all my life it has come up in two conversations: this one with Specter, and one other. But when I told Specter I was raised Catholic but then had left organized religion, he asked if I had been an altar boy, so I told him that I had indeed been until age 14, a bit unusually late.

After more than an hour the meeting drew to a close. As he stood to leave, Arlen Specter leaned in and said something personal to me. He told me that when he had been a federal prosecutor in Philadelphia, the toughest cases psychologically to investigate and prosecute were cases involved federal corruption. That was because, Specter said, "Over time, you start feeling like an enemy of your own government, of your own country."

I was perplexed that Specter had said that to me. I walked away surmising that Senator Specter was referring to the articles I had started penning and interviews I was giving on CNBC, talking about Wall Street's "regulatory capture" of the SEC. Only much later did I understand why Chairman Specter had said that to me as we parted. I have to laugh at the irony. Now DHS tells trainees that I am DHS Domestic Threat #1. So Specter's prediction has come true.

Byrne went on tell how that meeting changed his life. He says that a month later, he received a call asking him to come to DC. "Don't bring anyone, don't bring any lawyers," that is to say, those colleagues who had been accompanying him on previous visits to the Senate Judiciary.

Byrne went alone to DC and at the appointed hour went to the correct location. He walked into a room and found 7 Senators from both parties, waiting for him. Byrne describes what happened next.

Chairman Specter was de-transitioning to Democrat. Patrick Leahy of Vermont (Democrat) was part of this but he showed up about 10 minutes late. The junior senator from another New England state (because I am not 100% certain of the name of that Democrat, I am not identifying him, but I am 100% confident that it was a Democrat junior senator). There was also mention of one other Democrat: The name "Ted Kennedy" was used, but he was not there, and I did not catch if they were saying, "He is with this but could not be here," or were saying, "We tried to get him to agree but in the end we could not."

On the Republican side, there were Senators Hatch, Grassley, Crapo. and Kit Bond, who was not on Judiciary but was chair over on Intelligence.

In any case, they never sat down. These Senators all stood around as Chairman Specter repeated what I had been told all year, that the Senate Judiciary Committee is the "ultimate bulwark of the Constitution because its mandate includes stopping corruption, and therefore their power transcends every other power within government."

Then Specter said, "'we think you are right. There is some kind of corrupt forcing taking down our government. Some days it is like a foreign country doing it, other days not. It's everywhere. It's our job to stop but we can't stop it. We've seen that..."

I momentarily lost track as waves of relief washed over me. Until then, everyone had acted like they thought I was a nut, to be telling them there were cracks in the Wall Street settlement system, billions or trillions were being stolen, it would all melt down, and the SEC was asleep at the switch or else captured by the financial community it was supposed to regulate. The newspapers had run photos of me with UFO's coming out of my head, simply to suggest that Wall street had captured the SEC. It was a 'conspiracy theory,' they said. But now, after 18 months of banging my head on DC, Senate Judiciary from both side of the aisle had looked at the same data and whistle-blowers and insiders, and thought I was correct. Not just about Wall Street mischief, but also about the impression I had formed of Washington, DC. It was like surfacing after a logswim underwater.

Finally I interrupted Chairman Specter to gasp, 'I know! I know! This is what *I've* been saying. How do you even stop something like that?'

Specter said, "We are going to stop it because we have *you* and *you're* going to stop it." Hatch added, "That's why you're here." And the other senators around him nodded and joined in, adding, "Yeah yeah, that's why you're here."

They told me that the country needed me to disrupt that corruption. "They did not know how, they told me, and they said they might not be Senators when I finished, might not even be alive when I finished. But they needed me, the *country* needed me, to make this project my life's mission. Oddly, no one *asked* me anything. No one said, 'Would you be willing to do this?' They simply told me that the republic was done unless I agreed to do this for them.

Byrne was 43, and says that having seven US Senators from both parties standing around him telling him this was disorienting and intimidating.

"Specter said, 'We're going to be with the President tomorrow night and we are going to show him this letter. But it is going to be sitting the rest of your life in a safe in DC.' He held it up and I made as if to take it, but another Senator shouted, 'He cannot touch it!' So Senator Hatch held it and I bent over with my hands clasped behind my back and scanned it for about 15 seconds. It was 1.3 pages on Senate Judiciary Committee stationary."

Byrne says that the first paragraph spoke to the Judiciary Committee's concern over what it described as, "systemic infiltration of the federal institutions of our nation's government." And that that the second paragraph opened with words along the following lines: "The United States Senate Committee on the Judiciary requests that Patrick Byrne be afforded extraordinary latitude under the laws of the United States of America to investigate and disrupt corruption within the government."

According to Byrne, when he finished and straightened up, Chairman Arlen Specter said, "This is not a pardon, you cannot go kill anyone, but short of that, this is going to make it very unlikely any prosecutor ever touches you. We get that you're a bit different, Patrick, we get that you're a horse of a different color…"

The other Senators broke out in guffaws, "You sure are a horse of a different color!" and one made cuckoo motions with his finger around his ear, making everyone laugh.

"But we've come to know you, Patrick, and …we love you. We really love you." Seven senators stood around him nodding, muttering, "Yep we love you Patrick."

"Chairman Specter ended," says Byrne, "telling me that the country needed me to do this with my life, so that is what I was going to do."

Byrne says he pondered for several seconds before asking a question: "No take-backs?"

Seven senators stood around him laughing and saying, "Hahaha no take-bakes very funny haha no take-backs no take-backs!"

After thinking a few more seconds, Byrne recalls, he finally answered, "What can I say, Gentlemen? I won't let you down."

Byrne says that he then shook hands and had a word with each Senator. He says that one of the Senators told him that this had not been done in 65 years, but that during World War II there was a concern over German sympathizers within the government so a Wall Street man with contacts in government was asked to "become" a German sympathizer to flush the others out.

"Senator Grassley and I stood talking about his involvement in a matter I knew about, an SEC whistleblower named Gary Aguirre: Grassley seemed surprised and pleased that I knew about it. Crapo waited for me to say something, and I waited him to say something, until finally I just repeated, 'I won't let you down, Sir.' Kit Bond was not on Judiciary, but was Chair of Intelligence, and he was there to endorse the project. Senator Leahy and I spoke of my favorite moment in life: being 19 and tapping 400 maple trees on a Vermont hillside while up the road, Stubby Fullerton's sugar-shack spewed caramelized applewood smoke that filled the valley."

Byrne says this conversation happened in September 2006, on what he describes as an Indian summer's day. Asked if he knows how unlikely the story sounds, Byrne replies:

"Yes I do," says Byrne. "It probably checks all the boxes on megalomania with delusions of grandeur. All I can say is: it happened."

Byrne mentions that Trey Gowdy knows about the letter, for reasons Byrne will not explain. He claims that journalists including Matt Taibbi of *Rolling Stone* and Sheilah Kolhaktar of *New Yorker* have spoken with people who in 2006 were Senate Judiciary staffers, who have confirmed that a bizarre letter regarding Byrne does exist in the 2006 files. Byrne says that just a couple months ago someone he knows was visiting Grassley and asked about the letter, and that Grassley laughed and laughed, saying, "Yes we know Patrick, yes we remember that conversation, yes we are holding the letter." Byrne says that he has also heard that the DOJ has been wanting to indict him, but that Senate Judiciary Committee has been making clear that would be "a party foul," as Byrne calls it.

What if the Senate lets them indict you anyway?

Then I will consider that a take-back.

But that is all from 2006. Now let us get back to the 2016 story where we left it.

Please do. Where were we? In a room with three federal agents?

Yes. By February 2016, I figured out that I had being unwittingly used by the National Security apparatus in domestic political espionage. I knew with 98% confidence that they were using me

to manage Maria to smudge up the Republican Party and that someday they would pull the pin on that hand-grenade to create a massive Russia Scandal on the Republicans. Three federal agents had also had me set up an $18 million bribe for Hillary Clinton for purposes of a sting, but afterwards I learned that we had set up Hillary not for law enforcement purposes, but so that she could be blackmailed by Obama.

Byrne slows down and asks sincerely: "Now, I know that just because those names were used with me, it still does not mean anything. That world is such a Hall of Mirrors; there are people in that world whose names do not appear on an org chart anywhere. Whoever was behind this political espionage, let us call it, 'the Deep State' for convenience. The Deep State had tricked me into bribing Hillary Clinton so she could be blackmailed. The Deep State had tricked me into helping them use Maria to set up a 'Can-o'-Russia-Scandal' to spray all over Republicans.'"

"Someday I will be telling this story to 12 other citizens, good and true. So tell me, does that sound like 'systemic corruption infiltrating the federal institutions of our nation's government? "

Byrne seem genuinely curious. He is told that, if his story is true, it indeed would count as "systemic corruption of the government."

Byrne seems relieved. "That's good. Because I decided to avail myself of extraordinary latitude within the laws of the United States of America. I decided I was going to set-up my chain of command.... the moment I got a kill shot."

"The moment you got a kill shot"?

My Rabbi taught me this approach to life. Let me give you an example. My brother Mark was running a hedge fund, and Buffett put a lot of money into it. At one point Mark did a certain trade that Buffett liked, and he told Mark to lay it on big. Their prime broker, a large Wall Street bank, knew it was Buffett because of the scale, and took advantage by front-running the trade. It cost Buffett $100 million.

Mark was angry but Buffett told him not to be. He said, "When things like this happen, Mark, don't get angry. We're not going to say anything, we're going to wait for an opportunity, and then we're going to just *fuck* them." They waited until there was an even larger trade to put on, and Buffett had my brother place a small version of the trade with that bank, but the opposite of what he really wanted to do. The bank traded in front of it again, loading up on a position they thought they would be selling Buffett. Instead, through Mark and another bank Buffett moved big in the opposite direction and by the time the first crooked bank figured it out, it had lost $600 million to Buffett. That is how he teaches brokers not to game his trading.

I had been used to bribe and blackmail Hillary Clinton, the likely next president. I had been used to create a manufactured scandal linking Republicans to Russia. And whoever was behind it all had ordered my handlers to threaten my life to keep me silent.

Was I going to run to Loretta Lynch about all this? That's funny. For all I knew she was behind the whole thing. So I decided I was going to lay low, and when the right moment came and the universe gave me a shot, I was going to *fuck* everybody involved.

Because of your letter? That's crazy.

Well, you have not read that letter.

If you are suggesting that there might have been emotion attached to my decision, you may be correct. The *logic* of it was the letter. The Senate Judiciary Committee chairman told me our country was being taken over through some kind of corruption of our federal institutions and they were asking me to stop it So once the Bunson Burner was revealed to me, I had a duty to act.

But yes, there was also emotion involved. One federal agent representing John Brennan had threatened my life. Two FBI agents heard it, and looked at their shoes. As I said, they were aghast, like the same threat had been made against them, with a message to deliver it to me. But frankly, I think they may have looked aghast because they thought it was a really bad idea, to have been ordered to make the threat to me.

Let me explain: such meetings are practically hand-crafted. Before they meet with you, every aspect of the meeting has been scripted. Rehearsed, I think. There are shrinks back at HQ who know everything about you, who know you better than you know yourself. And when asked, I am confident that those psychologists said some version of: "'This guy is as Irish as Paddy's Pig. Don't threaten him. It will be counterproductive.'" Such people know to avoid threatening Irishmen or Sicilians, that you deal with them in other ways. Anyone who is street knows Irishmen and Sicilians respond poorly to being threatened. It's an honor thing. If someone threatens you and you take it, then you walk around the rest of your life as a punk. It is better to die than to be that kind of a man. An Arab once said to me. "A man without honor is a dead man anyway." That sums it up.

These agents knew me. *Had* known me for years. I could tell they either hated what they were doing, or thought it was a really bad idea. Maybe both.

Byrne says that given the Hillary bribery-and-Bunson-Burner story, the Russian "Can-O'- Scandal" setup, and the fact that his chain-of- command had just threatened his life over (he senses) the objection of his handlers, he felt he had found the "systemic corruption infiltrating our nation's government. So he did what he says any loyal American citizen would do.

Byrne says that after a few seconds thinking all that through, he grimaced and said, "Yes Sir, I understand, I will scrub every trace it from my memory, I promise..." While on the inside he was thinking, "I will blow this up on a world-historic scale... the moment I get a kill- shot."

"Make sense now?" Byrne finishes his explanation, apparently believing it makes sense.

Go ahead. How were you planning on doing that?

I did not know. That is what I mean by, "the moment I get a kill-shot." I was just going to keep my eyes open, keep looking, and when that opportunity came, incinerate them big-time. Bigger than Buffett thinks.

I don't mean to be arrogant, but think about it. Who do they think they are, threatening me?

I can tell you already it was not anyone at FBI. It was some political flunky somewhere making these calls, someone who is not on an org chart, or maybe someone in the National Security Council, someone who had seen too many movies, some want to-be gangster but who is not in the least bit street or else they would have understood (as my handlers understood) that threatening my life would be counterproductive.

Which brings us to the fourth and final part of the story. The first three were the set-up of the Russian Hoax, the setup of Hillary bribery- and-blackmail, and then the assignment from the 2006 Senate Judiciary committee. Now comes the fourth and final part of the story: "The Rape & Murder of Maria Butina."

"The Rape & Murder of Maria Butina"? She wasn't murdered. She is a member of the Russian Parliament today.

I know. She wasn't raped either. It was a setup. Just like Hillary's bribe and the Russian Hoax.

I hope you plan on unpacking this.

I told you how the FBI agents had spent 10 minutes teaching me about stings, right? How to avoid it being entrapment, a prosecutor has to show that there had been *predicate acts* (such as, "you pulled your car over at an intersection known for drug distribution, you put your car in park, you rolled down the window...") that establish that you already had the *prior disposition* to buy cocaine.

So when the undercover officer approached and offered you cocaine it was a solid sting, and not entrapment. Right?

Yes.

Well at this point in my story, whoever was calling the shots, let me avoid claiming it was Comey or Brennan because for all I know it was a "Deep State" of people not on any Org Chart. Well, this Deep State had had me facilitate an $18 million bribe for Hillary to lure her into a Snow Globe. This Deep State had had me get to know Maria not because they were considering having someone meet her, as they led me to think, but because they were constructing a "'Can-O'-Russian-Scandal'" to shake up, crack open, and spray on the Republicans (especially Cruz, Rubio, or Trump) any time they wanted. And that same shot-caller had just threatened my life.

Wouldn't you agree that those *predicate acts* establish that whoever was at the other end of my chain-of-command had a *prior disposition* to misuse the apparatus of our national security state to their own private ends?

When you put it that way, yes.

Ok then. By the power vested in me by the 2006 Senate Judiciary Committee, I decided to set them up in a sting.

What was the sting?

I did not know yet. But I was thinking of a torpedo the USA has in its arsenal. If we think there is a Russian sub off our East Coast, do you know that we have a torpedo that we can fly out in an airplane to that patch of ocean? We drop it, it hangs from a parachute, when it splashes down it releases the parachute and activates. Ping! Ping! It listens for the submarine, and when it hears it just goes homing in on it ping-PING-**PING**! .

I had my finger on the Launch button, and the next time the Deep State showed its wake I was going to lob a torpedo at it. No idea what it would look like. But I would keep my finger on the button.

Did the opportunity come?

Yes. Five months later. In the first week of July, 2016. For reference, the Republican Convention occurred in the last few days of July, 2016, but by the first few days of July it was clear that Trump was going to be the nominee. They sent word, we met, and they told me that I had been right about Russia, there were clear signs of Russian operations in the USA, they wished they had listened to me and not had me break up with Maria, Russia had become the highest level national emergency. They told me that the United States government normally does not do certain things, *never* does certain things, and this was one of them, and that I could refuse the tasking and no one would think less of me. But I was being asked to rekindle a romantic

relationship with Maria Butina, get back inside her head, and get to the bottom of anything she knewabout Russian activites in the USA. John Brennan and James Comey would be personally supervising the mission: the agents would be leaving meetings with me to go back to the office and report over video conference to Directors Brennan and Comey.

So I said to myself, *There's my kill-shot.*

What do you mean?

I saw a way to set them up on rape and murder.

You see, there was so much fake about their requests. How they had had me work Maria , allegedly to learn enough about her so they might agree to open doors for her in the foreign policy establishment. How they had had me breakup on the grounds that they had determined that she was just a normal grad student. How they were now coming back, acting all alarmed at realizing I had been correct and they should have listened to me.... It was all fake. I knew them asking me to get back with Maria had some purpose other what they were asking me. Nothing was right about the Russian matter and they told me Brennan was running the Russian matter. Nothing was right about the Hillary matter, and they had told me Comey was behind it. It was the opportunity to fire my torpedo for which I had been waiting.

So I decided on that spot that I would get the information they wanted. But I also decided that I was not going to lay a finger on Maria, I was going to treat Maria like she was the niece of Czar Nicholas II. I was going to be the most exquisite gentleman imaginable, in a manner that could be studied by prosecutors and historians. But I would give my chain of command a chance to implicate themselves in rape-and- murder. No one can spin rape-and-murder. As they would say at a craps table, "'it's a natural winner."

Shall I keep going?

Oh, please do.

I had been a jerk when I broke off with Maria the first time. I was extremely ill. As a matter of fact, back in that winter of 2016 I was Stage IV of two unrelated diseases at the same time. That may be why I got pulled into this: everyone thought I would be dead in months. Including me. So when they told me to break up I broke up and was abrupt about it, because I was sick.

So it took a couple months to get things rekindled with Maria. Soon we were communicating warmly, and I invited her out to Utah for the opening of a new building we had built for our HQ. As I recall, she spent a four-day weekend.

Here's the catch. When she arrived I told her that this time we were going to have an old-fashioned European courtship. When she visited she would sleep in the guest room. After six months she would decide: if she wanted to be with me, she would move to Utah, we would be married, and only

then would we sleep together again. She thought it was romantic and, since she was living with a Republican, it suited her conscience much more. Maria is really a very decent person.

So we spent 3-4 days getting reacquainted, going on drives, going to gun stores and shooting ranges, etc. But keeping things purely Platonic. And she is a great gal with whom to spend time.

[A jogger eyes Byrne in passing. Byrne waits a few moments before resuming.]

At the first opportunity I debriefed with my handlers. I told them I had deliberately gotten Maria inebriated, even wasted, questioned her, and could find no discrepancies. Just so you are aware, it is a bit edgy to talk that way regarding activities within the USA. Really, our people are clean. It is a disadvantage. Overseas, everyone is always trying to get each other drunk and talk. Maria was always trying to get me drunk and talk. But in the USA, our people don't condone that stuff. So as I said, it was a little edgy to say that I had done it on an assignment within the USA. I could tell it gave the agents pause. But they wrote it down with no repercussions.

Just as I was leaving they asked if we had been physical again, and I answered ith unusual machismo: "Yeah I'm back in the saddle, I shagged her all night long." It was out of character for such talk among us. Nothing like that had ever been said between us. It likely was a mistake. I was aiming to suggest that Maria meant nothing to me, but I probably overdid it: looking back, at least one of them registered a suspicious glance. I had my reasons, as you will see, but I overplayed it a bit.

We met again a week later for a more detailed briefing. I dropped clues that I had mapped out the night before. I did not describe the weekend in an organized manner as I normally would. Instead, I told it in fragments: there was the time we went to the gun range, there was this evening I made lobster linguine, and so forth. But I had designed it so that after I left the debriefing and they spent a few minutes fitting all their notes together, in a few minutes what would emerge is image: on the third day Maria had been with me I had taken her to a gun range, then on a drive, got her inebriated, taken her home, made her a romantic dinner and gotten her further inebriated, questioned her foran hour and found no discrepancy.... then had sex with her.

And there is a word for that, right?

Yes… and it is not a good word.

It's not. It is a horrible word. What is it? Say it.

"Sexual assault".

Correct. Try "rape". Once they put my clues together, they would be reporting on videoconference to Brennan and Comey that they believed I had gotten Maria Butina drunk, wasted, questioned her, then raped her.

Why?

Why? Because I wanted to see what Comey and Brennan would do.

OK, I'll bite: What did Brennan and Comey do?

They did nothing. That's what's so funny. The next time I met the agents, they had faces set in stone, they hated me … but they had clearly been ordered not to touch the subject, not to bring it up. Clearly in their video conference, Brennan and Comey had heard the previous report and told them, "Agents, don't you say a *goddamned* thing about it to Byrne. Don't you ask Byrne a single follow-up question on it.... If Byrne has drugged and raped Maria Butina, so be it. Just just let it go, we got more important things going on here. We got a Russian Hoax to set up here. We need Byrne and Maria for that." Get it?

You know something? They were right. The Senators who said you're a horse of a different color, that you are extreme. They had your number.

Yeah I get that a lot.

So I waited another meeting or two… then I offered to murder Maria Butina.

Actually, I worked it all out then waited until they brought it up again. At one meeting they said, "The folks back East want to know if you can really do this without falling in love."

I told them, word-for-word: "Nietzsche said, 'Philosophers don't really fall in love: it would be like seeing tiny, delicate hands on a Cyclops.' Can you imagine that, a monster with tiny, delicate hands, how silly that would be? You tell the folks back East that if they send word, I'll cut this chick's head off and bury her in the Utah desert, nobody will know a thing.'"

I am pleased to report that three federal agents jumped to their feet into gunfighters' crouches. One clicked-out of his holster momentarily, then put his weapon back and wagged a finger in my face as he stood towering over me in my chair. "Let's get one thing perfectly clear, Byrne. *We* don't care what orders come down from DC. If you harm a hair on Maria's head, we're going to kill you ourselves." All three looked at each other and nodded curtly at me, to suggest the subject had already been discussed and agreed upon.

I am really happy to report that, and I swear on my eyes they did it. It was exactly the right thing to say. I am really confident these agents were not bad men, but like me had been tricked into the situation we were in. Yes they conveyed a death threat to me, but they were all family men, and I am sure they thought they had no way out themselves. But they worked for bad people, and like me had not realized it. I think we all found out the same day how we had been used.

[Byrne cups his hands cupped behind his head.]

But you see: I had to box in the Deep State. I had realized that I was on a path working for people, whoever they were, who were trying to take over the government of the United States through political espionage. I didn't know who it was, though I knew the names used to get me to play my role. But I knew I had bribed Hillary for what turned out to be blackmail. And I knew I had been used in the setup of a fake Russian scandal. And my life had been threatened if I opened my mouth. That was the path I was on.

So metaphorically, I chopped a tree down across that path. I put whoever was running the coup in the following position: either they had to stop the coup they were setting up and whatever role they had written for Maria to play in it… or someone would have to sign-off on the aggravated rape and possible murder of an innocent woman that never happened.

What happened?

Someone signed off on the aggravated rape and possible murder of an innocent woman that never happened. Then they had me date her for five more months. Yuck yuck yuck yuck.

After six months she told me she *did* want to move to Utah and be with me. I was told to end it again, on the grounds that, "We are learning so much watching her move around DC, seeing who she is having dinners with."

So I broke off. Just like that. You get why?

At this point, we're afraid to guess.

Because ultimately, what was my assignment? My *real* assignment was this: in 2006, some 300 million Americans chose a Senate, which chose a Senate Judiciary Committee, which chose a chairman, who told me their power transcended every other power within government, some kind of corrupt force was taking over the US government and that they I was going to disrupt it for them.

So the more corrupt the orders, the better. My assignment for the Senate demanded I go along with the most corrupt orders of the Deep State. My assignment *demanded* I do it to *find* the Deep State. Maria was my perfect opportunity for that.

Remember how I said that I saw Maria as 60% opportunity for something good (increasing peace between Russia and the USA),

30% risk (because she was swanking around with our politicians while connected to Russian senators), and 10% something else?

Yes.

That 10% is what I am talking about now.

In high school wrestling and football we used to use plastic mouth guards. One would get a new one each season, drop it into boiling water, bite into the soft plastic for a minute, and have a custom mouth guard.

I regret to say that as impressed with and fond of Maria as I was, in a sense she was that mouth guard. By 2015 I had reasons to believe something deeply corrupt was going on within our government. I cannot explain why, but I had been bumping my head against the Deep State since about 2010. Too many opportunities missed, too many decisions made no sense. I did not know what exactly, I did not even know how to explain it back then.

But Maria came along and she represented a perfect opportunity: she was a blank mouth guard. *She seems to want to be dropped into the national security pot, so let's do it and see what the Deep State does with her.* It would be a perfect opportunity to show the American people what's what. I knew we would be getting a perfect dental impression of the Deep State. Which fulfills the tasking from the Senate Judiciary Committee.

In other words, when I first reported Maria 10% of me was thinking: "Let's see how they handle this Maria situation. If my hunch is correct, I will end up with a perfect dental impression of the Deep State to show America. That's 'Mission Accomplished' I think."

So how did it play out?

After they thought I had drugged, raped, formed a plan to murder Maria and proposed I do it, they thought I was on board with them. They decided I was *really* one of their boys. They had me continue seeing her for 5 months, then break off so she would stay in Washington going out to dinner with Republicans and posting photos of it on Facebook.

Then, 15 months later, as the Russian Collusion narrative reached a frenzy, around the time that people were to starting to ask why this Russian scandal did not seem to have any actual *Russians* in it… the day that Presidents Trump and Putin met, just a few hours before they met, an FBI SWAT team and a CNN van descended on Maria's boyfriend's apartment in DC to arrest her.

For the next year, night after night on TV it was photos of "alleged Russian spy Maria Butina," a striking Russian redhead with sniper rifle and thigh-high leather boots. Hollywood Central Casting for a Russian spy. That clip of "accused spy Maria Butina asking Donald Trump a question in Las Vegas" played 1,000 times on the news. Over and over, to associate the two of them.

Eventually a federal prosecutor argued in a courtroom for 15 years in prison for Maria, on the grounds that grave damage was done to our national security by Maria having those dinners around DC with Republicans and posting it on Facebook… all of them being ones the federals knew about, often before they happened, sometimes from me, and occasionally *created* by me, like the Chrystie meeting.

From the day Maria arrived in July 2015, it was all as "producer-driven" as the Spice Girls.

A couple years ago in an interview with the Wondery podcast, Peter Strzok said something to the effect, *You really want to know what made us open Crossfire Hurricane in July 2016? We learned about Maria Butina! That's why it started.*

That is a flat lie. They learned about her in July of 2015, and played cat-and-mouse games with her for a year. That's not a theory. I am a participant. A witness. I did it. He is lying. They are lying.

Incidentally, the Senate Intel Report about all of this a vacuous nothing-burger.

The Durham Report gets correct what happened after July 2016, but covers up all of this, so it is only 50% cover-up.

So... you tricked federal officials into signing off on rape and murder? Couldn't you have gone with something less horrible?

No no. Rape-and-murder was great. Rape-and-murder was *perfect*. First, because it was the opportunity that presented itself. Second, because it was the start of the Weinstein era. They had been playing games with me since the start: since the day I first reported Maria I knew they had me operating within some big con they were playing. I knew it was mischief of a kind, but I could not suss out what. But I decided after the Hillary bribery-and- blackmail caper that it was up to me to nail them and I had a duty to nail them. I knew I was going to sting them, but did not know how. It was like being the slowest man on a kickoff team, having to make that clutch tackle.

So when they came back and asked me to re-seduce Maria, it was a perfect opportunity to create a rape-murder gambit on them on which they'd have to sign off to continue what they were engineering.

It was beautiful. You know why? Because it's tough to spin rape-and-murder. These guys spin everything else. Bribery and laptops and recordings and videotapes... but you can't spin rape-and-murder. It was the opportunity that came my way and it was perfect.

Why aren't you in prison?

Four years ago, I walked into the DOJ and explained all of this. The first thing they told me was that I was in a lot of trouble if Maria did not corroborate my story. I told them I was not in the least worried, go talk to Maria. They asked me why I was so confident, and I told them that Maria is a Woman of Steel, that no matter that she was then sitting in a box, and knew I had something to do with it, still she would tell the truth. You would have to know Maria to understand why I was so confident.

They next day they interviewed Maria in her box. She told them what she told Sara Carter shortly thereafter, when Sara Carter interviewed Maria in prison. **[Byrne switches into a Russian accent]** "I have never met such a gentleman as Patrick Byrne! Yes that first time we dated was physical but the second time we saw each other Patrick was the most perfect gentleman with me! I did not understand a man could be so kind. He flew me in jets and helicopters, beautiful restaurants... but he insisted I sleep in the guest room. He did not lay a finger on me. I did not know such gentlemen still existed...!'"

Four years ago the DOJ and Sara Carter confirmed this all. That first period Maria and I dated was ... *wonderful*... but the second time I treated he as untouchable as a Romanov princess. I just reported crazy shit up my chain of command to see how wed they were to the coup we were working on together.

You know how wed they were? Turns out they were rape-and-murder wed. Turns out that to accomplish their political espionage, they'd go along with rape-and-murder. Yuck yuck yuck yuck.

Happy Birthday America! That's your Deep State.

I know this story may sound odd to people who do not know me. But there are probably still dozens of people around DC who knew me in high school. You could ask any one of them, "Is Patrick Byrne the kind of guy who, if he figured out the Directors of the FBI and CIA were running a soft-coup to take over the US government, would compromise them in a rape-and-murder sting of his own design?" I promise, the answer you will get from 10 out of 10 is, "Yeah that's Pat." Some may e v e n say, "You could have told me the story without the name, and I could have told you, 'Oh you're talking about Pat Byrne, right?'"

Why is that? You think you're a saint?

No not at all. I am the farthest thing from a saint. You know, when Gandhi died, Orwell wrote an essay on him, "Notes on Gandhi". In it he wrote, *Many men do not aspire to be saints, and some who aspire to be saints never felt much temptation to be men.* I am definitely on the "'man" side of the line. It is more that... well you'd have to ask them.

We'd like your thoughts.

[Byrne ponders for some moments]

People find me quirky. 15 years ago I had dinner with Susan Sarandon and Tim Robbins. It was a year or two before they split. Halfway through dinner, Tim said something funny to me.

Remember how I mentioned that the Arlen Specter conversation was the first of two conversations in my life that I had cause to remember I had been an altar boy?

Yes.

This dinner with Tim Robbins and Susan Sarandon was the second. Halfway through dinner Tim said, "You were an altar boy, weren't you?" I told him he was correct, and asked how he knew. "You have a quirkiness about you. Sometimes men who were altar boys have that specific quirkiness, and you have it, man.'" I told him that some people, including myself, think Tim Robbins is a little quirky. He said that was because he had been an altar boy too. He told me that if as I go through life and note men who have that same quirkiness as he and I have, I will often find that it is men who have been altar boys.

So think of the quirkiness of Tim Robbins. It is that characteristic. To me it is funny that someone thought it would be OK to tell me that we just destroyed America and I had to keep my mouth shut or be killed, and it would end there with me. It's really funny. [**Byrne guffaws**] It's hilarious, actually.

It was a strange observation of Tim Robbins to make. But he was right. Smart actors like Tim are astute observers of the human condition.

Anyway, enough about bribery-blackmail-rape-and-murder. If you want to find out who set up RussiaGate, who set up the Hillary Bribery-and-Blackmail-Hoax, and who thought it would be productive to send me a death threat, find out who signed off on the rape-and- murder of Maria Butina so the Russian project could continue. Find that out and you will find who is behind a lot that has happened since as well, perhaps.

What do you mean by that?

It moves into the realm of speculation. Let us stick with specific , concrete claims.

OK. What was it like to have been proven right on Wall Street after three years of press abuse?

There is a Zen story about a monk who loves being a monk. One day a village girl gets pregnant, and she tells town-folk that the monk is the father. The villagers come and berate the monk, "You horrible man. How could we have trusted you around our children?!?" The monk calmly replies, "Is that so?" He takes the baby, raises it as his own. The villagers always tell him, "We will never forget, you horrible man, we trusted you!" Each time he calmly replies, "Is that so?" After a couple years, filled with remorse, the girl explains that someone else is the

father, but he dodged so she accused the monk because she knew he would do the honorable thing. The people come to him apologizing, "How could we have thought those horrible things about you?" The Monk calmly answers, "Is that so?"

PBS calls you the "kingpin" of the election integrity movement, which some people claim is insurrectionist by nature, a threat to democracy.

A claim which no one will explain to me.

We'd love to understand how you came to be here. And, as you know, one question that is frequently asked is, "Where is the evidence?"

"Where is the evidence?" That's funny. When I hear it I want to say, "They keep it in the same attic they kept Hunter Biden's laptop and Joe's $10 million Burisma bribe.

Since November 4, 2020 a tremendous amount of evidence has been all around us. 75% of the public sees it, and whether or not they can articulate it, they sense it. But 25% of the public is so brainwashed they cannot see it. I will show you what I mean by answering your other question first: how did I get from ejecting from my company, going public about my role in the Russian Hoax, and dipping to Indonesia... How did I get from there to the middle of this? Let me answer that first.

Go ahead.

I came back from Indonesia because I received instructions to do so. I was in a far out-of-the-way island, sleeping in a hut at a surf camp. I got a message one day, "We can kill you wherever you are, it doesn't matter that you're in" and named the little village I was in. At first I was hesitant, replying that I thought I would be arrested or killed if I returned. I would not come back until a federal I knew sent me a thumb's up. Days later, I received photos of federal people I recognized giving a thumb's up. One of them was William Barr, sitting at his desk with the Washington Monument framed in the window behind him, with one hand holding up a *Washington Post* to show what day it was, and the other giving a thumb's up.

Attorney General William Barr.

Correct. So I came back early. Early 2020, or maybe late 2019. I was directed to support a counter-trafficking activity that was spinning up. Covid hit and all went to ground for a few months. Meanwhile, I had a tumor growing on my spinal cord that reached the point one leg went paralyzed. I could not walk. That took microsurgery and a month of recovery. By August 2020 I was back. There was a counter-human trafficking activity going on. Some people involved were cyber guys, 'dolphin-speakers' as I call them, who turn out to be useful when disrupting human-trafficking networks. Some of those dolphin-speakers were making a hobby out of studying election fraud.

This was August, 2020. They walked me through vulnerabilities in the machines' architecture, hardware, and software. They steered me to YouTube videos showing how easy the machines were to hack, videos since removed as "misinformation." Along with an HBO documentary called "Kill Chain" that is now also *samizdat* ***[Byrne uses the Soviet term for 'banned literature & art']***. More importantly, they downloaded operating manuals and sales brochures from the firms themselves. There was also a study done by California's Secretary of State in 2007, a woman if I recall. She formed a commission of computer scientists from UC Berkeley, Stanford, JPL, etc. to study these systems. They concluded the technology was garbage. Junk-ola. It violated basic tenets of computer security. So bad, it may have been *designed* to be vulnerable, they wrote.

They clued me in on election scandals occurring globally. Philippines in 2010 and 2016, Ukraine 2014, Iraq 2008, Ghana, Kenya and other African nations... In each of these cases, there was interruption in ballot- counting for one reason or another, then when counting resum

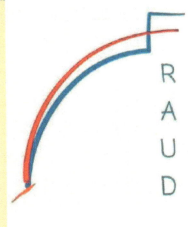

Last year, June 2022, the DHS issued a report that could have been titled, 'Patrick Byrne Was Right Again. Again.' They listed nine major security lapses in a brand of machines. Read   report. It represents my state of knowledge on about October 20, 2020:

https://www.deepcapture.com/2022/06/dhs-issue-report-patrick-byrne-was-right-again-again/

Two weeks later was the election. Ballot counting stopped. For the first time in US history, a city just stopped counting ballots. How odd.

And it was not just one city, it was six. How odd.

And it was not just *any* six cities, it was six anchor cities for six swing states. Cities with 2/3 of their state's vote. How odd.

So the Mainstream Media says, "Where's the evidence?" That *is* evidence. No one has ever tried to explain it, really. Six different cities, six different   but what do you kno   They each flip a swing state   ch flips the electora college. Which flips the White House. And they all decide to do this first-in-America event of stopping ballot-counting on the same night? Seem odd?

You see, there are about 3,000 counties in America. On Election Day, we really hold 3,000 separate elections. To steal the White House one does not need "'widespread election fraud'": one needs deep election fraud in six counties, each of which is roughly 2/3 of the vote of a swing state. That narrow, deep fraud flips those swing states, and flipping those swing states flips the electoral college, which flips the White House.

And what do you know? That set of six cities in six swing states... are the six cities that stopped ballot- counting! How odd. You get it?

So the improbability of that constellation of events is one layer of evidence from 30,000 feet.

    we go down to 10,000 feet: statistical improbabili es in outcomes. The stuff Seth Keshel finds. 18 of 19 "bell-whether counties" voting for Trump. Things like that. Things like... Did you know tha   2020 more Black people voted for Biden t   ted for Obama? I always knew Black folk *liked* Barack Obama, but it turns out they are just *wild* for Joe Biden... But only in Philadelphia and a handful of other cities. Does that   ible?

Perhaps you   mean, "Where is evidence of systemic misconduct in the conduct of the election?"

Within a day or two of the election I was in Washington DC setting up rooms with researchers and dolphin-speakers. I knew that whatever legal process came along, at the end of the day, lawyers could do no more than write each other memos until there were researchers and dolphin-speakers surfacing facts and data. Because I was the first in the country to go on TV and put his name on the claim that the 2020 election was rigged,

soon I had groups trying to find me in DC. Sending delegations to find me.

It turned out that in many states, so many people experienced such irregularities that citizens quickly found each other, grassroots groups just started swirling into existence, electing leaders who themselves started gathering evidence and gathering affidavits, and assembling teams in their own states to do it. Then they were flying to DC and finding me.

I set up debriefing teams with retired military and law enforcement. Evidence was assembled, piped up the Legal. Rudy and Sidney and others they wanted to have it. Then... I do not want to bayonet the wounded. But as I made clear in

what I wrote later, trying to work with that legal layer and the White House was (as a Master Chief we met at the time said) like watching a half-dozen monkeys try to fuck a football.

At first I thought I'd never seen anything like it, but in time I realized that I had seen things just like it before: any time I've seen a group of lawyers in charge of a project. As an entrepreneur watching a lawyers try to organize to accomplish something under stress... I cannot describe how unbearable it was. Given that I knew the deeper significance of what was going on, that this was a stage in a psyop to take- down the United States, it was a nightmare. They clearly saw me just as some rich guy on the side who had agreed to write the checks, and they had no sense of how to work with someone like me to create a fluid, agile, task-oriented enterprise. There were these stunning assets, there were people sending up information, there was a White House scrambling, but between the two there was a layer of lawyers, and they had their priorities, which included meetings with no agendas, and endless bull sessions discussing past triumphs, and their own internal jockeying amongst each other for court favor, and podcasts, and positioning things so they could take the credit, and so on and so forth. I saw the days ticking by and this disorganized shitshow going off half-cocked over and over. Rudy's press conferences about Joe Frazier voting, Sidney filing cases that I doubt she even read, filled with typographical errors. Trump being told many different things by the most mediocre intermediaries.

What was your famous December 18 Oval Office meeting really about, and is it true you snuck into the Oval Office?

True-ish.

The first thing you need to know is that in the autumn of 2020, the US Government made a number of statements.

On October 9, DHS published its annual report, "Threats to the Homeland," and early in the report it identified our elections as high on the list of targets of foreign powers.

But on October 21-22, DHS and FBI came out with a public statement: Our election systems are under attack from hostile foreign actors, particularly Iran.

On November 3, they came out with an updated statement: Iran has successfully hacked one state's election rolls, are going after others, and other hostile powers have joined in.

On December 6 they put out a warning about a massive cyber-attack occurring against the USA.

And on December 13, DHS-FBI-DNI came out with an announcement that the USA... how shall I put it... had been hacked straight through to the teats. Of the Fortune 500 companies, 425 were hacked, along with CIA-DOD-NSA-DHS-State-and-so-on-and-so- forth across the federal government, because they all used a network security product called "SolarWinds Orion".

The next thing you need to know about is that in 2015 President Obama signed an executive order which said, *If a foreign government interferes in an election, the President has a range of powers, from running a quick investigation, to a Presidential Commission, to re-running the election in that precinct, county, or state. Really, if foreign governments interfere in an election, the President can do pretty much anything the hell he wants to sort it out.* Obama signed an EO that said that in 2015. And in 2018, President Trump renewed it, or signed something else quite similar.

Once that December 13 DNI statement came out, there were enough statements from the federal government that it tripped the prerogatives of the Executive Orders of Obama and Trump. Our argument had precisely 0 to do with theories of vote-flipping from space, or South Korean jets flying in ballots, or any of these claims that mainstream media parade as being ridiculous. That was all beside the point. The statements of the federal government *itself* were enough to trip the executive order. Once the December 13 SolarWinds statement came out, General Flynn, Sidney, and I all saw that.

We wanted to go make that case. I guess it was difficult to get a time to see President Trump. Finally around 6 PM on Friday, December 18th, I called a couple staffers I had gotten to know, reminded them they had been inviting me for a White House tour, and told them I wanted to take them up on it, right then. Somewhat confusedly, they agreed to meet me by the White house gate in 30 minutes. I went up and told General Flynn and Ms. Powell that we had an appointment at the White House, perhaps leaving them with an impression it was with someone other than two staffers. Only when we got over and inside the gates, and met them, did the situation become clear, perhaps. In any case, from there we improvised around the Executive Office building and then the West Wing until we got down the hall from the Oval Office. President Trump walked by the open door, still dressed in an uncreased suit and a blue tie at 7:30 PM. He saw me down the hall in a motorcycle jacket, Lululemon shirt, and jeans, looked startled... then General Flynn and Sidney stepped around the corner and the President waved us down.

I think that counts as, "Yes." In any case, what happened when you met?

Sidney took the lead on familiarizing him with the Executive Orders. As each was presented he stopped the talking, studied the EO in question for perhaps 60 seconds, then continued, showing full understanding. He's a quick study, I am saying. I had not expected that to be so readily apparent.

General Flynn and Sidney together presented the statements from the federal government itself. We did not have the October 9 DHS annual report printed, but we had a folder with each of the other federal announcements in it. Again, Trump took each in turn and scanned it, then asked Mike about it, who answered with occasional input from Sidney. Zero percent, and I mean *zero* percent, of what was presented had anything to do with stuff you have heard about, South Korean jets flying in ballots and such. It was all straight out of

government statements. And reviewing a couple executive orders. Finally President Trump picked up the last document, an action plan of several pages we were asking him to sign. Out of the range of options the Obama/Trump EO gave, we were recommending the lightest footprint option: a quickie investigation to be conducted in two weeks by the DHS.

That was the only document that President Trump did not read, but just glanced at, then looked up confused and said, "So what are you asking me to do?"

At that point I spoke up for the first time. "Put us in, Coach. Put us in. We'll get to the bottom of this." He indicated for me to continue.

I told him that if he accepted our argument that Executive Orders were triggered by these federal statements themselves, we were asking him to take the most light-footprint option, and order a quick investigation. If he did so, there would three choices for him to make, and with each choice, a spectrum of options from light - footprintto heavy- handed.

I paused to give President Trump time to process, which he did, then nodded to continue. The first question is, "Where is to be investigated?" There, Sir, your choices are 6, 13, or 31 counties. The obvious 6 that shut down counting. But there are 13 that look suspect. But we have also selected a total of 31 if you want, a mix of rural, urban, and suburb, Democrat, Republican, White, Black,

Hispanic, that will let us answer that question political scientists have wondered about forever: how much fraud is there in US elections?

Trump immediately beckoned towards the low end of the spectrum I had laid out with my hands, saying, "No no, go with 6."

The second question is, "What is to be investigated?" We could have ballots recounted on livestream TV. We could image hard drives in the machines in those six counties and take them back to government facilities for inspection. We could *remove* hard drives and take them back to a government facility for inspection. Or we can *remove entire systems* and take them back to government facilities for inspection. The last would be most complete, but the truth is, Sir, if we image the hard-drives it is about 80% as good as everything else, and far less intrusive.

President Trump again beckoned towards the light end of the spectrum I had laid out with my hands, indicating the image-the-hard-drives option.

The third question is, "Who is to do it? Sir, It could be the DHS FBI, or the DHS." **[In the document we gave Trump it was written as "DHS" but I went off-script.]** Please consider the possibility that what we are experiencing is a breakdown in social trust in a core institution. I am not sure the FBI and DHS are all that trusted now. I know that there is a taboo of involving the military in elections, but please consider the possibility of using Federal Marshalls

bolted to National Guard cyber-teams. I understand that there are strong cyber capabilities in the National Guard. The judiciary and military are the most trusted institutions in society: the Marshalls work for the Courts and the National Guard are "citizen soldiers" from all around us. Using them would be the quickest way to reinject trust into the situation.

To his minor credit, the President's lawyer, Pat Cippolone, waited until I finished, then spoke for the first time. He said something like, Mr. *President, the public will come unglued if they see any uniforms involved.* He made a 30 second argument.

The president turned to Rudy and Mark Meadows, who had been on the speakerphone throughout. They each took 20 seconds to echo those thoughts. The President turned to General Flynn to ask his opinion. Mike was thoughtful for a moment, then said, "The DHS has units that are perfectly adequate for this."

Trump turned back to me and said, "OK, DHS."

I broke protocol (I learned later) by re-pitching my case. I said, "Sir, it is your call of course, but..." then asked him to reconsider the collapse in trust, individual US Marshalls bolted to small National Guard Cyber teams...

Trump cut me off: "No uniforms."

So three decisions were made by Trump, each with the lightest footprint possible.

At that point I said: "Mr. President, that document says we can have this done in two weeks. Tonight is December 18: if you sign it, we can have an answer for the nation by New Year's Eve. But the truth is, we will have an answer in a week, we think. And the real truth is, we will be able to tell you in a few days if we are finding what we expect to find. And Sir, if we do not, I think you are going to have to concede immediately-"

President Trump cut me off to say, "Pat, you have no idea how easy that is going to be. I will have no problem doing that. Right over there *[He turned from the Resolute Desk and pointed out the window at the South Lawn of the White House]* on January 20, Marine One is going to land. I can walk out of here and fly away knowing I accomplished more in four years than has ever been done. I will *never* spend another day in this city again. I've got my golf courses, I've got my friends... believe me Pat, my life is going to get a *lot* better. But if I think this election has been stolen...,and there are foreign nations involved...how can I do that? Can I really do that?"

In my view Trump's moral reflection was entirely appropriate. Everyone knew what novel Constitutional moments we were living that evening, and everyone in the room conducted themselves like it could have been recorded and played for posterity. But Trump's moral anguish was particularly highlighted for me. He correctly believed it had been rigged, and he thought he might be surrendering the country if he did nothing about it. I emphasize this because the false narrative has been that he was some tyrant clutching at power. Just the opposite was true: he personally was half-longing to be done with Washington, I think. But he was torn from a sense of duty, and by the confusion of the days, as were so many.

The only mention of January 6 that evening was me, pointing out, "Sir, you don't have to sign this tonight. You may want to study and think. But you cannot wait past New Year's to sign it, because it will take us at least a few days to execute. In any case, please know I think you cannot wait until January 6 and, if things do not go your way, ask us to do it. That would be 'sore- loserism'." Trump nodded in agreement.

There was also a point we were half-alone, moving through a doorway together. He stopped, leaned in close to me for emphasis: "Pat, I mean it, you have *no idea* how easy it is going to be for me to get on that helicopter. I'm going to be with my friends, I'm going to be golfing, I am going to be enjoying my life... I'll have no problem walking to that helicopter. But how can I do that if I think this was rigged and other nations are behind it?"

What happened then?

Well I have recounted the substance. Much of the meeting was repeated for two more hours up in his residence. It turns out that after we left, in two minutes Rudy Giuliani turned him around, told him *We will all end up in prison if we go ahead with Byrne's plan.*

If that is what that happened, why didn't others tell that to the J6 Committee? Why did anyone take the Fifth?

The way it works is, once you go under oath if they ask you, "How do you like the weather?" and you answer, then when they ask you legal questions looking to nail you and you try to take the Fifth, they say, "You already answered some questions, you cannot pick and choose." I may be exaggerating but not by much.

Others had legal privileges to maintain. Some have had enough DOJ trauma to want to avoid more.

And you?

Not me. I'm in my prime.

You know, I spent $50k taking out ads around Washington telling the J6 Committee to have me in. I'd come in under oath, no lawyer, and answer all their questions. They dodged me for nine months before finally having me in. I told them all that I have told you. I heard later that the lead investigator, a Marc Harris, decent enough fellow, tells people that the J6 investigation fizzled because, "Patrick Byrne covered for Trump." The truth is I did not "cover for Trump," I told the precise truth. But the truth put a hatchet in the head of the fake narrative they were trying to create.

What was the narrative you think they were trying to create?

That there had been a color revolution planned, we were there to brief it to Trump, and J6 was an outgrowth of that. That's 100% delusional. As was the "military seizing voting machines across the nation." The plan was DHS cyber-teams imaging hard-drives in six counties for later analysis at government facilities. The only mention of "military" was *me* proposing the National Guard plus Federal Marshalls instead of DHS, which was immediately rejected by everyone in the room including General Flynn, and shot-down twice by Trump. The only mention of J6 was *also* me, in the context that Trump should not wait until J6 then activate our investigation.

What can they charge Trump with? He saw me outside his office, beckoned me in, listened for four hours, and decided against me. What can they charge anyone else with? I am the one who yenta'd the meeting together. I was the one who briefed the options.

As I've explained, 300 million Americans signed a letter asking me to stop the "systemic corruption infiltrating our federal government." I'm happy to meet the DOJ in any court in the land and defend my actions. Charge me first. Plus, I had my mental GoPro running, and think history should know the truth about exactly what went down.

Anyway... So perhaps you meant, "Where is the forensic evidence ?" Well, re- counting pieces of paper gets nowhere. To find out if each of those ballots came from a legitimate voter requires examination of the electronics. Regarding that, the same people who ask, 'Where is the evidence?' are the people who since November 4, 2020 have fought teeth-toes-and-fingernails to make it impossible to examine evidence.

Remember, all that has to be done is examine hard drives from 6 places where ballot-counting stopped for three hours. Each for a different reason, each for three hours. The investigation could be done in a week. This whole battle ripping our country apart could be solved with a week's work. But for two years, five of those six counties have legally blocked having their hard drives inspected. *That's evidence.* To a guy who solves problems and not just opines from lofty heights, their opposition to inspection of hard drives is evidence. They make cockamamie claims that inspecting those hard- drives would be a threat to democracy, or a crime against nature, but no one explains why.

The sixth city, Phoenix, Arizona, which is to say, Maricopa County... The Arizona Senate issued a subpoena for their hard drive, along with lots of other things. Maricopa County fought the subpoena for six months. *That is evidence.*

Then a court finally *ordered* them to turn it over and they could no longer stall, the night before they turned it over they erased it. *That behavior is evidence.* Then six months later, when they were challenged for having erased the data, they said that they had not actually erased it, they had duplicated it then deleted it...but when asked for the duplicate, they refused to turn that over. *That is evidence.* In any normal period of our history, such behavior would long ago have been decisive in the court of public opinion.

Didn't the Maricopa Audit show Biden won?

That is the biggest lie I have ever seen the press selling the gullible. First of all, in any normal world, once they deleted the hard-drive they failed the audit. "Failed: Deletion of Records" is what that is called. The auditors could have just stopped there because after that there was actually no way to audit the election. Not really. They could hold sheets of paper up to lights and such, but there was no way to unscramble which ballots were legitimate and which not.

Setting that aside, what they found was that while Biden "'won" ' by 10,800 votes:

- **The ballots did not reconcile:**

  - 255,326 Early Votes had no provenance (but simply "appeared");
  - 284,412 had digital images that have been corrupted (with no explanation for how that happened);

- 57,734 ballots had sourcing that is illegal (e.g., they were mailed to someone who had moved out of state 10 years ago, but were voted anyway);
- Over 17,000 ballots were photocopies (which are unambiguously illegal);

• The day before complying with the subpoena, Maricopa deleted > 1 million election files (each deletion carries 1 federal and 1 state charge unless it is against Trump);

• 15 other felonies occurred whose impact on the ballots is impossible to quantify;

If we turn a blind eye to all of that, yes Biden wins by 10,800 votes. But 600,000 ballots had violated Arizona and federal law.

In addition, the recent Kari Lake trial exposed that in the 2020 election Maricopa received 1.2 million mail-in ballots, and accepted every single one. Maricopa certified that they examined every signature on those 1.2 million ballots and they were all good. How does one estimate what 1.2 million ballots without a single signature rejection mean for an election? How many would they normally reject?

Does the fact that none were rejected mean that Maricopa skipped its duty to verify signatures? If so, did others know beforehand that this was their plan, and take advantage of it? How much did THAT effect the votes? One cannot estimate. You can't unscramble this egg.

It is a sign of either how idiotic or corrupt the media is that in the face of all that, they say, "But where's the evidence?' Or that, "See, Biden still won by 10,800!" An honest representation would be that the audit showed there were 600,000 dubious ballots, and 1.2 million mail-ins without a single rejection, but if we count them all, then Biden wins by 10,800.

All over the nation, citizens have discovered that for the first time that, attempting to inspect election equipment or processes is suspect, or even makes one a Domestic Terrorist, and in some places gets one criminally charged.

In Grand Junction, Colorado, the County Recorder, an apolitical grandmother who took the job because she was concerned about a backlog of parking ticket collections, a citizen just trying to do the right thing, got wind that people from State were coming to wipe out election data that it was her duty to maintain. Under federal law, materials from elections have to be preserved for 22 months. Everything: every hard-drive, thumb drive, email, every scrap of paper they ticked-and-tied on. Every file or document erasedis its own federal felony.

Yet goons from State came and erased 100,000 files in this Colorado town.

Fortunately, unbeknownst to the bad guys, the County Recorder had caused a friend of mine, a court-certified forensic cyber guy, to come make an image of County's hard drive before State's goons arrived. So that if State's goons broke the law and erased what was on the drive from elections in 2020 and 2021, a backup would be available.

Afterwards an analysis was prepared by two experts, one a Professor Emeritus of Computer Science from Texas A&M, the other, the CEO of a cyber-security firm. Their report was called,

"Mesa County Forensic Report #3".

They discovered two things on the image:

• There was a massive cram-down of 100,000 files by the folks from State, which is 100,000 federal felonies and 100,000 state felonies (unless Trump);

• The town's 2020 election had indeed been altered. After a quarter of the 100,000 votes had been tallied, a hidden script woke up, created a new (illegal) database, siphoned over 24,000 ballots but 30,000 showed up, and the provenance of at least 6,000 is unclear.

Remember those old photos of Black people in Mississippi trying to vote, and facing Sheriff's deputies with German Shepherds keeping them away? How horrible a period of America history, that some citizens were so dehumanized? When election fraud happens because they inject 6,000 fake votes, there are 6,000 actual citizens whose votes are cancelled, correct? So it is like 6,000 people being held at bay with German Shepherds from the voting booth. This disenfranchisement is just as horrible. It is simply done differently.

You know who is being charged with a crime for this? The County Recorder, the grandmother who had the duty to keep her county's data safe. Even though she had the duty, and even though the law specifically says she had the power to make a backup, they are trying to put her in prison for 25 years. One felony on the grounds that she gave a badge to a non-County person (my certified cyber-guy), another for letting him into County's computer center, one for lying so that those people she suspected of corruption would not know that she was imaging the hard-drive so as to be able to catch them if they smashed-down the data, which they did.

It's Kafkaesque. But it is a warning to those who might stand against corruption.

[Byrne rubs the new scar on his neck.]

So out of one side of their mouth they say, "Where's the evidence?" while from the other, "No one is allowed to examine any evidence!"

In reality, everywhere that there has been access, it has revealed so much slop, so much infidelity to law, bureaucrats not bothering to follow the law…. they don't even bother trying to appear like follow the law anymore. Look at Maricopa's 2022 election. On Election Day 60% of machines failed. Expert witnesses found the failures were programmed into those m,achines. Of those bad machines, 93% were put in Republican voting precincts. As George Carlin once said, "You don't have to be Fellini to figure this out."

There is evidence in the manuals of the machines, there is evidence in the ballot-counting stoppages, there is the mathematical evidence, there is forensic evidence anywhere people have had a chance to inspect. And there is behavorial evidence in how the Establishment has broken all previously known rules in covering this up. Unless you are living under a rock, you see the evidence.

But that is for another day. I promise, I am as correct about our election systems as I was about Wall Street settlement 15 years ago. Someday that will be understood.

Why couldn't the government find the evidence in late 2020?

I will tell you what I know: Administrations are structured so that the White House has what is in effect an ambassador to each of the Departments and Agencies of the federal government. The liaison from Trump to the DOJ at that moment was a seasoned, mature woman, known in DC as a serious person. November 4, the morning after the election, she went over to the DOJ and confronted General Barr, asking the question on the minds of hundreds of millions of Americans.

The day after the shit-show that was Election Day 2020, an election that included six big swing-state cities stopping their counting at once, she asked: what are you going to do about this, Bill?

Barr told her, *The DOJ is not getting involved.*

Once the grassroots folks had found me and so much information was coming at me, and it had reached some semblance of structure, I called Barr's office and let them know I wanted to come talk to someone with what we had already accumulated. I received back only a message: if you have any information of election malfeasance in a state, contact the US Attorney of that state.

I tried contacting the offices of three US attorneys: not one returned the call.

There is a man from Pennsylvania, William McSwain, who at that time was US Attorney for Pennsylvania. He has come out and said that he received stand down orders from William Barr on conducting any federal investigation into what had happened. Recently Judicial Watch revealed that they FOIA'ed DOJ/FBI notes and records of all DOJ/FBI investigations into Election 2020, and the response came back: after a thorough search, there are no notes or records of any interviews or investigations. None.

Which is odd, because at that time, Barr was saying that they conducted dozens of investigations with hundreds of interviews and could find no evidence of any widespread election fraud. So that is odd.

You know what is also odd?

Barr saying that there was no "widespread election fraud." Barr is a smart guy: he knows that there does not have to be, "widespread election fraud." That is a straw-man argument.

There needs only be fraud that is narrow and deep, primarily in six counties. So the fact that he would even utter such a sentence tells me he was not interested in the truth.

Why do you think William Barr did that?

I will tell you what I know. There was someone going back and forth between us with messages and information. In June of 2020, William Barr sent me a message to me that ended, if such and such doesn't happen, *"We will be meeting in a FEMA camp by the summer of 2021."*

Barr sent you that in June, 2020?

Indeed he did. But then our intermediary made a visit to me on the last day of July, and in the course of other conversations he told me that in a week Barr was going up to New York to see Rupert Murdoch and they were going to spend three hours together alone.

The next day that intermediary was killed in a cross-country plane crash with an instructor on-board, flying to see someone who works with me. That looked suspicious. A week later, somebody who survived the crash got out of the hospital and an hour later sat for an interview with me (I'm a 1,500 hour twin engine pilot). His story of how the crash occurred hung together for me. Still, I understand there remains federal suspicion about it and they may be right. My understanding is that this death devastated General Barr. I will say no more.

But if a historian goes back and looks at Fox broadcasts in August 2020, that historian will see that in the middle of the month Fox got what I can only describe as a soft-off for Donald Trump. Damned with faint praise, or damned with no praise at all. Fox was still Fox, but its editorial tone altered in mid-August 2020. And then there was the issue of them calling Arizona for Biden when the data did not yet support the call.

So Barr went in June 2020 from fearing that totalitarians were attempting a revolution and that if we did not defeat it we would be meeting in a FEMA Camp by summer 2021. Then at the beginning of August there was a death. Then a meeting with Murdoch in early August, 2020, and later in August, Fox shifts its editorial tone markedly. And once the fake election came, with irregularities orders of magnitude beyond anything America had ever experienced, Barr shrugs it off to the White House, lets them know he would not be lifting a finger. And orders (per McSwain) all US Attorneys not to investigate irregularities, but to leave it to states. Refuses to let his office meet me to hear about RICO patterns we had already found and tells me to go to the states , who won't return calls. Yet later claims he did "dozens of investigations and hundreds of interviews," while later FOIA shows that they did 0 investigations and 0 interviews. Barr also publicly said they found "no widespread election fraud" which is a meaningless, straw-man thing to say anyway (and suggests he looked, which is also a lie, as FOIA revealed).

Connect those dots as you see fit.

Now let me move on from the election and get to something more urgent. Are you ready?

You have stories that top that?

In 2021, it was made known to me that there were still people looking out for me. Over time it was gradually revealed to me that there was an interagency team of some sort, spread across a dozen agencies, that had become the hot ticket within the three letter agencies, a group of super-agents, O-5 and O-6 level, who were in an interagency group dedicated to reverse engineering the international attack against the USA. I came to think of them as a "League of Shadows" who were looking out for me.

In September 2021 the Iranian government reached out asking to see me. This is why I told you as much about our relationship as I did earlier. Iran contacted me again and let me know a big war was coming, and their call to me had something to do with peace.

I stalled them, and let the League of Shadows know about it, letting them know I was reluctant to get involved but I would do as directed. It was only at that point that they revealed themselves to me in person. They studied it for some weeks, then instructed me to accept the offer to meet. I specifically confirmed, "You have checked with X, you have checked with Y?" They confirmed they had checked with everyone and it had been signed off on across-the-board.

So in November 2021, I went back to the Middle East. I met with a group including a very special Iranian figure, an old friend who let me know a World War was coming, and had a proposal to avert it. I told them I would relay the proposal but I did not think it would fly.

In the course of being there, and through a mechanism I am not going to explain here, I became aware of an additional situation. Hunter Biden was reaching out to the Iranian government in the fall of 2021 with the following offer: "You Iranians have $8 billion frozen in a bank account in South Korea. My father will unfreeze it in return for $800 million being funneled into a numbered account for us. And if you do this deal with us, it will lubricate other negotiations which have recently started between us." By that, the Iranians believed that Hunter meant the JCPOA talks, which had restarted in Geneva a month or two previously. In other words, something along the lines of, "Pay us $100 million and we let you keep 10 nukes, $200 million for 20 nukes," etc. But I am making up the pricing.

Hunter was doing this through a middleman, the son of the Minister of Defense of Pakistan. That son was meeting with Hunter, then relaying messages to someone in Iran. And he was being reckless enough to leave voicemails in Iran about it.

When I returned, the agencies went to work over the weekend. I was told a week later that they had confirmed it all. The voice on the voicemail that I had acquired was voice-matched to the son of the Minister of Defense of Pakistan, who had a connection to Hunter Biden. Anyway, in December, 2021, I was told that the scheme was confirmed across the agencies.

Patrick, you are claiming that 18 months ago, the Biden Family was seeking a bribe from Iran to release funds frozen in South Korea, and to go easy in nuclear talks, and that the United States Government has been aware of this since December, 2021?

That is 100% correct.

Now let me move on to the second event of four.

There are hacker activists around the country. They use their cyber skills to further some cause. Sometimes they are called, "hacktivists".

One group of such hacktivists is called "Blue Leaks". They are transsexual Democrat hacker activists. They helped the J6 committee do face recognition, for example. But believe it or not, within the transsexual Democratic Party hacker activists there is a subset who are *patriotic* transsexual Democratic Party hacker activists. And they started dealing with someone in the

Dark Web that they understood could safely get material into the hands of the United States government. They started funneling to that person some stuff having to do with blackmail. They did so with the understanding that it was going to be brought into the most incorruptible cell within government. It is possible they understood it was me but I am not certain.

I let the League of Shadows know I had no idea what was on these drives. I insisted they confirm they understood there could be absolutely anything on these drives: could be nuclear secrets, could be snuff films, could be kiddie porn. There are certain things where there is no word in any language that excuses you for having it on your computer.

Eventually I was told to retrieve and courier it whatever it was. It turned out to be horrible.

[Byrne seems lost in thought for a moment.]

One piece showed that Perkins Coie had not simply directed its computer scientists in Georgia to plant information on Trump's server that would connect him to a Russian bank called "AlphaBank". In addition, the Perkins Coie computer scientists tried to plant kiddie-porn on Trump's email server. To do so they went to some Ukrainian kiddie-porn websites and obtained kiddie-porn to inject on Trump.

As I said above: there is no word in any language… yet here, Perkins Coie's computer scientists were grabbing kiddie porn on their computers. To plant on Trump.

A second thing: I was given forensic information that a foreign adversary had hacked the VA Medical System. I knew the name of the country and even the individual within the VA who opened a back-door for them. I have hesitated a long time to make this public: I did not want to be the source of any Vets going off their pills. But there *was* a breach. Since the government has had over a year to process this, presumably the breach is pugged now. No Vets should go off their medications. But the VA Medical system was hacked in 2021.

Lastly, there had been a breach of US Government Fusion Centers across the Southeast. There were files of what looked like 100-200 people, their passports and names. I was told they were the dossiers of various undercover federal agents. When I presented it all to a 30 year federal agent, he looked through it and told me he recognized half a dozen of them as feds with whom he had worked. The transsexual hackers had recovered it out of the Deep Web, where it was for sale.

There were a couple more loads, mostly material that fit into these categories.

In addition, dolphin-speakers communicated to me that the version of Hunter Biden's laptop that Rudy Giuliani had obtained and copied was incomplete. Hunter had BleachBit 400,000 files before turning his machine into the Delaware computer repair shop. Unbeknownst to the world, however, there is a way to recover information even after it has been BleachBit, if the right dolphin-speaker gets the hard drive or a forensic image of it.

The right dolphin-speaker had gotten a forensic image of it. The missing 400,000 files included signature pages of contracts Hunter had erased before turning his laptop into the repair shop, as well as texts from Hunter's phone that had been backed-up on the laptop but had also been BleachBit. Those texts filled in a lot of missing pieces. I also gave it to the League of Shadows. A forensic image of Hunter Biden's laptop.

Somewhere in there news broke that the FBI had "'lost'" Hunter Biden's laptop. That is another half- truth. They may have "lost" the physical laptop but they have a forensic image of the hard-drive, including 400,000 files he deleted with BleachBit that my cyber-friend recovered. They have it from me.

Eventually they got word back to me: "'Did you keep a copy of that hard drive with Perkins Coie kiddie porn, VA hack, and the Fusion Centers?'" I had not, of course. But it seemed an odd question. I came to suspect that Director Wray and General Garland caused the hard drive that I had sent to be destroyed. Perhaps Wray stood in the room when it was nuked in FBI laboratory's machine.

That would be discouraging, if an FBI Director were destroying evidence. That would make him a dirty cop.

I realized that was going to happen to all I had couriered for them. So I sent instructions to the hacktivists, including the patriotic transsexual Democrat Party hacker activists, to prepare another copy of their information.

That portion that dealt with the forensically complete image of Hunter Biden's laptop I caused to reach Garrett Zeigler, a young man whom I met in the White House. He had started his "'Marco Polo'" operation, but was unique among those looking into Hunter Biden's drive to have the full version, including the worst 400,000 files Hunter erased just before turning his laptop in.

I took the 2.5 Terabytes of the other stuff I mentioned, and caused copies to be stored in safe places. For when we have a functioning United States government again...

My understanding is that the information I brought in, particularly the stuff linking Perkins Coie to kiddie-porn, was so radioactive that the leadership of this immensely successful inter-agency task force, one that had operated for several years with great success, which had gotten large budget increases, and was considered the hot ticket in each of a dozen three-letter agencies... the leadership was called in and fired,

or sent home on suspension. The interagency task force was disbanded, and agents got reassigned around the country. Two decided, "Screw this" and walked into Congress as whistleblowers. Then six. Then a dozen. Then 20. Then 100. Then hundreds.... Remember hearing about that last summer? I have spoken to members of Congress of late who say they are so swamped with federal whistleblowers they do not have enough staff to handle them all.

I think the first snowflakes in that avalanche of federal whistle-blowers we've been hearing about were from that high-speed team dealing with me. And they brought into Congress the stuff I have been telling you about here. Along with, no doubt, other stuff they had seen on their own.

We have reached the point where the United States Government is what in MMA they call "a fighter who is no longer intelligently defending himself." So they were doing the right thing to go to Congress. The owners of the government, We the People, need to know that our government has jumped its tracks. And I am right to tell the public about it.

There are two last things to tell you. To understand them , you need to know that sometimes whistle-blowers reach out to me. I hate mentioning that because my experience is that anytime I do, no matter how I do it, more people do.

So let me be clear: **I want no more whistleblowers ever to reach out to me ever again in my life. Please: never again.**

OK, with that said… two sets of whistleblowers reached out to me. One came through a fancy, high-end lawyer in DC. His client worked at CIA, maybe CIA security. The lawyer delivered to me this detailed message: In 2015 CIA Director John Brennan had visited the UK, and had visited Moscow. On the visit to the UK, Director Brennan had slipped his security and been seen in the back of a limousine where he rode for 3 hours. It was believed that the head of the UK branch of the FSB (which used to be called, "KGB") was in the limousine.

Later, in April 2015, Brennan went to Moscow. He slipped out of the US Embassy at 3:30 AM and got in the back of a limousine in which he rode for 2.5 hours. It was thought the Director of the Russian FSB was in that limo.

That is interesting on many levels, but here is one reason. This was never mentioned in the US from what I saw, but according to what Maria told me, she had first visited the USA in *March* of 2015, not July. She was on a delegation with the Central Bank of Russia, acting as assistant to the Vice Chairman of the Central Bank, Senator Alexander Torshin.

From the story I told earlier, you understand that since November 2015 I was clear that they were plotting a Russian Hoax. But I said I guessed

the possibility for the first time in September, 2015. And given when their out-of-character behavior started, in retrospect saw that it may have been as early as *July* of 2015 that they were planning it, and that is why their responses to me were out of character.

But consider this hypothesis (and this is no more than speculation). Imagine this is what happened:

In March 2015, Maria Butina visits the US for the first time as part of a Russian Central Bank delegation. She gets noticed. I promise, there is no way she would not be noticed. I have not dwelled on it, but let me explain more fully.

Maria Butina is an extraordinary human. Russia still has a system (a holdover from Soviet days) where they test every 6 year old across the nation for mental and physical superiority, and send the top 30 kids to a special school for 10 years. Maria was selected and spent 10 years there, graduating #2. She has university and master's degrees in political science, knows our liberty tradition better than almost any American I know, talks fluently about Locke and Milton Friedman and Bitcoin. She is also a physical specimen: champion power lifter, runner, kick-boxer. General Mikhail Kalashnikov at age 93, practically on his deathbed, selected this 23- year- old girl to lead the organization he founded. She did her Masters at American University in Washington while all this was going on, and I saw her transcript: it was a couple dozen A+.

That alone should tell any but the most historically illiterate that she is indeed an extremely special young woman.

My point is, when in March 2015 Maria Butina was in Washington with the Russian Central Bank, there is *no way* she was not noticed before she flew home. And if I got that whistleblower's information correct, then it was the following month, April 2015, that Brennan went to Moscow and in the wee hours slipped into a limousine with Russian FSB.

Consider the possibility that what he said in the back of that limousine was, "Hey last month you had this red-head intellectual over in DC. Send her back to DC and we'll have some fun with her."

In May, 2015, Maria gets asked by Russian Central Bank Vice Chair/Senator Alexander Torshin to come to America to do graduate studies, try to build relationships into Camps Hillary, Cruz, Rubio, and Trump. Maria, bright-eyed idealistic graduate student of political philosophy, dreaming of playing a role in bringing about peace, agrees.

In July, 2015 Maria comes over, flies directly to Las Vegas. Asks Trump a question. Then goes on to DC to live with her Republican boyfriend and schmooze around political circles, bright-eyed at the possibility of being a "'citizen diplomat'" playing a role in nudging the world towards peace. An idealist who lets people know within 10 minutes of meeting them that she is connected to powerful players in Russia, not hiding her hope to be part of some thawing of relations. Having dinners and posting it on Facebook. Not knowing that from Day 1 the entire thing is being observed and managed by Brennan in the background.

If this hypothesis is true, it means the Russian Hoax did not start in September 2015 or even July 2015. It started in *April*, 2015.

As I said, that is only speculation. But if it happened that way, that is interesting for this reason: it was two months before Trump came down an escalator and declared his candidacy. Which confirms it was just part of constructing the elements of a coup on whomever came to power, like bribing Hillary Clinton so that she could be blackmailed.

What went wrong with that plan was the day Maria landed in the USA, in Las Vegas, she heard my keynote and sought me out. And ended up sharing not just her invitation but her intentions, not knowing my relationships meant I needed to report it. Why?

• Because I *could have* opened doors into think-tank's within foreign policy circles and elsewhere, but I would first need to get a thumb's- up;

- Because I held a security clearance, and was being invited to Russia;

- Because I was worried about her talk of schmoozing around our political class;

- Because I wanted to witness whatever was done with this *tabula rasa*.

From their indecisive response, I suspected they were cooking something up. Certainly as early as September 2015, maybe as early as July 2015. And if my story about Brennan and the limousine is true, it was April 2015. Before Trump announced.

Meaning: the Russian Scandal was set up so that whoever emerged within the Republicans was going to slam into a Russian scandal. It was not about Trump at all.

Even if this hypothesis fails, I can promise, in the July-September 2015 timeframe (*not* 2016) tthey were definitely setting it up on Cruz, Rubio, and Trump. And anyone else who emerged on that side of the aisle.

What you know now is the truth. A Congressional Committee could verify every word of this in 48 hours if they wanted to. The difference between it and what you have previously been told is a measure of how corrupt our systems are. The DOJ, the Mueller Commission, the Durham Report, the Media. It has all been a 7 year corrupt charade.

This is a lot to take in.

I am sure. But I have one final story on corruption.

People within the DOD and Law Enforcement communities reached out and found me for the same reason others find me. **Again, please, no whistle-blowers ever call me again.** But they found me and began communicating with me about a situation.

There is a recent book called, *Code Over Country: The Tragedy and Corruption of SEAL Team 6*, by Mathew Cole. You must read it. It claims that within the Navy SEAL community there has been a rogue element, particularly within Team 6 since its days under Marcinko. Eventually leadership came along that formalized it, managed its brand, and built an organization where a large number of honest, patriotic SEALs are unwittingly shielding the existence of a small cadre of criminals.

How this came about was explained to me: there is a certain SEAL from Delaware who went to the same high school as Biden, and of whom there is evidence of contact with Biden in his youth. This man corrupted SEAL Team 6, so the story went. Then after 9/11, laws were passed encouraging agencies to hire from Seal Team 6 and similar units: bad actors from within Team 6, as well as clean ones, got sprinkled across the agencies. There the bad ones have come to act as a Praetorian Guard for the Deep State. More specifically, like a late Roman Empire Praetorian Guard, one that not just *guards* the emperor, but *chooses* the emperor. This Praetorian Guard has been protecting the Biden-Clinton nexus of corruption. Not all SEAL Team 6. Just an element within.

That is what this network explained to me over a series of interactions.

I got this into the hands of the League of Shadows. Soon thereafter, the man in question, who had risen to a high rank within SOCOM, resigned his position.

10 days later, that book appeared, *Code over Country*. Mathew Cole seems to have known some insiders, too.

I am sure the majority of SEALs, including SEAL Team 6, are great Americans. Heroes. But there are some who are not, and they have worked themselves into every three-letter agency in government. It is a massive CI problem that needs to be studied. I will stop there.

How about we throw some quick questions at you, for your comment?

Sounds good.

Are we living through a revolution?

At one level, yes, "Maoism with American Characteristics," as I explained. But more fundamentally, you are living through a Bezmenov Model Psyop.

I hope you're going to explain that.

A Bezmenov Psyop is a way of taking over a country without firing a shot. It comes in four stages: Demoralization, Disorientation, Crisis, and Normalization. The idea is to demoralize and weaken the target's population, then get them so disoriented the world seems psychotic to them, then force a crisis down their throat, then say, "The only way back to sane normal reality is to accept what just happened."

For us, "Demoralization" was Covid-19. The response to Covid-19 was unserious from a scientific point of view in two ways. The first way it was not based on science was the denial of early treatment, and the second way was its attachment to the "Woke-Poke" vaccine.

Covid-19 received no early treatment. Ask any doctor to name an upper respiratory virus that when the patient presents at the hospital and tests positive , the patient is told, "Go home, rest, come back if it gets bad." They don't. Patients are given antibiotics to avoid bacterial pneumonia, anti-inflammatories, in some cases drugs that prevent viral replication.

But Covid-19? "Go home and have some chicken soup, come back if your lips turn blue."

DARPA has leaked that CDC and FDA knew in 2006 that Ivermectin, HCQ, and Zinc worked on Sars-1. Covid-19 is the disease that comes from Sars-2, which differs genetically by 23%. It could have been snuffed out with Ivermectin, Zinc, and HCQ in weeks, as some nations did.

Also, the mania about vaccines was unbearable. Vaccines need long-term testing, especially when they rewrite human DNA. It does not matter how many billions of people you test for a few months, you still have zero long-term results.

There is a famous book in computer science, *The Mythical Man-Month*. New managers who learn that a software project will take 4 people 10 months often think, "Well that is 4 X 10 = 40 man-months. But 20 X 2 = 40, so I will just throw 20 people at it and get it done in 2 months." In fact when they throw 20 people at it they find it takes 2 *years*, because the coordination cost increase outweighs the horsepower increase.

Similarly, it does not matter how many people you test for 3 months, you do not have any long-term results. You can test a billion people for three months, and you can't say, "We have 3 billion months of testing!" You still know *zero* about long-term effects.

The response to the pandemic was unscientific because the pandemic was necessary for social separation. Anxiety. "Demoralization."

"Disorientation" was the Antifa/BLM stuff. Taking over six city blocks of an American city and nobody doing anything about it. "Mostly peaceful protests" that injured 1,000 police and killed 33. In October 2020 I was walking in DC near the FBI building when a bunch of leather-clad guys on motorcycles and ATVs took over the street in front of the FBI. They did donuts and wheelies for 10 minutes in front of what is putatively the world's premier law enforcement organization. Unmolested. No one lifted a finger to stop them. After 10 minutes they drove away.

These happened to tell you, "This is not the America you know, it's a new world you've entered."

"Crisis"? That was the rigged election. I won't go into it again.

"Normalization"? That's Cancel Culture. They want to prohibit opposing viewpoints. That is because they have done so much evil to seize power, they want no one to criticize it. Also, their ideas are bad and cannot stand on their own.

These last few years in the USA have seemed strange, with censorship, and Antifa, and crazy elections, and a pandemic. For most people it seems like a kaleidoscope. If you consider the Bezmenov paradigm, you will see that they fit together as four pieces of a puzzle: Demoralization (Covid), Disorientation (Antifa/BLM), Crisis (Election 2020), Normalization (Cancel Culture).

Are we going to find evidence of fraud in election 2020 from those cases that are finally moving forward?

Yes. Before the next election.

Are you afraid of being killed?

If they blow me up I win.

Seriously? Nothing else you feel about it?

I've died 500 times. What's 501?

What if they throw you in prison?

Tell them to send my ass somewhere I ain't been before. Like Hawaii.

Sorry. That's something funny I heard someone say 47 years ago. I won't lie. I would not like it. Other the other hand, that is why I took up yoga a decade ago: I wanted something I could do in a prison cell.

What if the Senate Judiciary does not back you up?

Then I would consider that a take-back. And see if I will ever do something like THIS for them again. **[Byrne laughs]**. Honestly, I have been hearing for over a year that General Garland wants to indict me, but that Senate Judiciary has told him that would be a party foul. I was in ambiguous circumstances, and I knew Hillary was setup only so she could be blackmailed, and I had seen the Russian Hoax cooked up for about a year, and they had threatened my life. Only then did I launch my rape-and-murder torpedo.

I was sent to be in that position 17 years ago by 7 Senators who stood around me and told me they needed me to make it my life's work to disrupt the "systemic corruption infiltrating the federal institutions of our nation's government." They asked me to find them the Deep State, I found them the Deep State. And, per their instructions, I didn't kill anyone. I just implicated them in a rape-and-murder that never happened. Specter is laughing from his grave.

So to sum up, if I understand you correctly, you are claiming that the Deep State tricked you into setting up Hillary Clinton so they could blackmail her. And the Deep State tricked you into setting up Maria Butina and the Russian Scandal. But you figured it out and boxed them in: to continue their political espionage, someone had to sign a piece of paper instructing your handlers to ignore their belief that you had drugged, raped, and planned on and offered to murder Maria Butina?

Yes. Exactly.

Were you going to kill her if they asked?

Of course not. Are you crazy? I had two routes to get her out of the country and on her way home, if they told me to kill her. But I knew they would not: there was no point to it. They had their own plans for her.

The point was for me to make the offer. That was the sting. There was no way it was going to slide. It was going to be like that torpedo-from-a-parachute we use against Russia. It was going to find its way to the depths of the Deep State and present someone with a dilemma.

Did it work?

In the summer of 2020, they confirmed that they had found Hillary's bribe. A government guy came to me with a photo of a statement from a bank in Azerbaijan with a numbered account holding $18 million. I was told it had arrived in late January 2016, just as I had told them they would find.

So I asked the federal, "How did my rape/murder gambit play?"

The federal winced, and told me that the three agents had put my clues together not in the minutes after I left the room, but in 10 seconds, They went back to the office and recommended scrubbing the mission. They were overruled.

"Then Patrick," he said (having trouble saying the words), "after you offered to eh-heh-heh *murder* Ms. Butina, they went back to their office and *demanded* it be killed."

"But it wasn't. It went on five more months."

"Someone else took all responsibility," he said.

That happened, when?

October 2016. The month Trump got in trouble for his "You can grab them by the pussy" comment. That same month, I put the Deep State in the position of, to continue their coup, they had to sign off on a rape and murder that never happened. After that, they had me date her five more months, breakup, and then a year later, the moment they needed their Russia Hoax prop, just hours before Trump met Putin, they arrested Maria. Ruined that meeting of Trump and Putin. That is the Deep State conducting foreign policy. They knew everything about her for three years, they knew every zigzag, but they arrest her that day? Then they kept her in a box the size of my shower stall. No windows. A mail slot they opened three times per day and slid a bowl of mush to her. 18 months.

You remember that American college kid who went to North Korea and did something frat-boy? He stole a poster of Great Leader in a hotel elevator. They sent him home three years later howling from a burlap sack, and he died in days?

What the Deep State did to Maria wasnot quite that bad, but close. In their eyes, she was manipulated, seduced, drugged, raped, by a guy planning to murder her (me), as she was being set up to be the perfect prop for the day they pulled the pin on the Russia Hoax, so they could keep her in a box for 18 months feeding her mush through a mail slot. That way they had one actual Russian to whom to point when anyone said, "Why doesn't your Russian Collusion Drama have any actual *Russians* in it?"

Now the seduction drugging rape and murder was all fabrication, but the Deep State did not know that. The prosecutorial setup was real, and the 18 months in a box eating mush through a mail slot was real. Find out who was behind that, and you will find out who is behind these events.

What if it was Barack Obama?

I hope it is not President Obama. It would definitely hurt my feelings if it were he.

Did you vote for him?

No, I did not vote for President Obama. Either time. Nor Trump for that matter, either time. Nowadays journalists assume that I am a Trumplican, always write it. I vote libertarian, and always have. Partially because I truly am a "libertarian republican," as Milton put it, though I don't think the Libertarian Party is anything special. But also, because of these requests I never wanted to be associated with either side. But for both Obama and Trump, when they won, I served with equal enthusiasm. I was not keen on some of Obama's policies, but I loved Obama's style. And I thought Michelle was a super-classy First Lady. I knew our politics overlapped but were not congruent, but of course one sets that aside.

I had more congruency with Trump's policies, less with his style. But you know what? The way the Establishment lost their minds about him, Trump grew on me.

Why do you say it would hurt your feelings if Obama was behind this?

There are things that I thought would go to my grave with me... But here we are. I did two things for President Obama before this other stuff occurred. One might consider them dangerous. So I would be disappointed if it turned out he sent me a death-threat through my handlers.

Can you say what they were?

No, not really. I am not supposed to anyway. I never expected it to appear in my lifetime. But I have been put in a rather bleak situation, and I have to clean this up. I will reveal as little as possible but that lets me still make my point.

The first was the first week Obama was in office. I was called to a government facility, briefed on a tasking and told that it was at his request. I was to make my way a country where there was no US Ambassador, make contact with the head of their Gestapo, and do a certain thing they needed done. I did it.

Again, why would they ask you to do that?

Because he was an old friend of mine.

Obama?

No. The head of the Gestapo.

Why was the Gestapo an old friend of yours?

We're never going to get anywhere if I have to keep going backwards. He was an old friend of mine, so I was sent to make contact and make something happen they wanted to happen. I did.

The second regarded an issue in the Middle East. My dad was dying. I was on my way to spend his last Christmas with him. I got a phone call. These things are never done by phone, but I got a phone call from Gregory Craig. He said he had retired as White House General Counsel a few days previously and gave me a way to verify him. I did. He told me there was a missing American, he was running the administration's response, the computers said there was someone who was friends with a certain senior Al Qaeda cleric, "...and it's you, Patrick Byrne. Is this true?"

I said "friends" is a big word but I could deal safely.

He told me my task, which necessitated getting in touch with various Bad Guys in that world, including that cleric. I asked who was sending the order, and he gave me some government names, but ended: "I'm looking through the trees of Lafayette Park at the White House, at the window to the living quarters of the White House, at the man asking you to do to do this."

So I did it. Instead of spending my dad's last Christmas with him. He died shortly thereafter. You know the core media team of ISIS? The one that does the beheading videos, the pilots-burning-alive-in-cages videos? They have a photo taken on Christmas Day, 2012, in an apartment in a slum in the south of Giza, Egypt. The four of them standing arm-in-arm of this tall American guy, jean jacket. That is I. That is what I was doing on Christmas Day 2012 instead of being with my pop on his last Christmas, because President Obama needed something done. Just as in early 2009 I was in another place at his request.

You asked why my feelings would be hurt if the orders to setup Hillary and engineer the Russian Hoax were from him? Or if the death threat I received was from him? That is why.

So you're saying the core media team of ISIS has a selfie with you, Patrick?

Indeed they do. But to be scrupulously honest, they were Al Qaeda when I was with them. Six weeks later they defected from Al Qaeda to Raqqaa, Syria to join ISIS. But they treated me honorably.

We have had it confirmed that you indeed have these requests made of you. Can you share any more explanation?

I've told you what I know.

You know that old Western, *Jeremiah Johnson*? There's a scene where Robert Redford finds a settler woman, her family has been butchered and she's keening by the bodies. Redford gets things sorted out, buries the children, fixes the woman's cabin, sets her up with supplies, as she keens for days, talking to the ghosts of her children. As he leaves he tells her, "The Injuns will leave you alone now, Woman, because you are... touched."

I smust s e e m mentally handicapped, because all my life, wherever I go people are kind and look out for me. Even Al Qaeda and ISIS. Go figure.

Did you love Maria Butina?

Well to some degree, that thing about "a Cyclops with tiny, delicate hands" is true. So it was not a question of love. You could certainly say that I was fond of her, deeply fond of her. I felt a tremendous admiration for her. I think she is extraordinary woman: brilliant, athletic, liberty-minded. Can talk Austrian Economics like Ron Paul. It did not seem strange to learn that at 93, General Mikhail Kalashnikov choose her, branded her with his name, at 23. So smart and well-read that when she, at 26 years old, sat with me describing her aspiration to be president of Russia, it did not seem strange at all. I've been around some good universities, known a bunch of smart kids, I've even taught a few smart kids here and there... Maria is remarkable.

At no point did Maria or I think in terms of, "We should be together someday." I think we admired each other and were grateful to spend time together, her Kalashnikov's girl, me Milton Friedman's guy, but I wanted to see her on her way to become president of Russia. Believe me, Russia could do far worse. In fact, Russia has *done* far worse. For about 800 years.

But in 2006, as delusional as it sounds, 300 million Americans elected a Senate, which chose a Senate Judiciary Committee, which chose a chairman. He and at least half a dozen of his colleagues from both sides of the aisle told me their committee's power transcended every power within the United States, there was some kind of "systemic corruption infiltrating the federal institutions of our nation's government," and they wanted me to disrupt it. Maria represented the perfect opportunity to do that.

At one point, her name appeared in an article as a Russian grad student swanking around with big shots in DC. I tried to tell her to walk over to the FBI, declare herself, and say, "You may have read things about me being here and have concerns. May I answer any questions that you have?" I never revealed more than that to her. I told her she did not have to be disloyal to Russia, but since her name was in the papers she should clear up any misunderstandings with FBI before they got out of hand. She told me that as a loyal Russian she could never do it.

It's not much, but I did try to make use of her in a way that would benefit her and her greater goals. I thought that if things went bad, she might have to do a couple nights in jail then would be sent back to Russia a national hero. On her way to the Duma. I had everything correct but the "couple nights in jail," which turned out to be 18 months in a box.

There is a movie I thought of as I was doing this, an under-appreciated movie called "Mad Dog & Glory" with Robert De Niro, Bill Murray, and Uma Thurman. De Niro is a wimpy police photographer, so wimpy the cops call him "Mad Dog" with irony. In a liquor store shootout he saves the life of a vicious gangster, Bill Murray. In gratitude, Murray befriends De Niro, and tells him he wants to be the "facilitator of all your dreams." In time, De Niro confesses his great dream was to be a tough guy, fighting bad guys, saving the girl. Instead he is a wimpy police photographer.

In gratitude for saving his life, Gangster Bill Murray loans him one of his girls, Uma Thurman, with whom De Niro falls in love, of course. When Bill Murray comes one day to take her back, De Niro must... you guessed it... be a tough guy, fight the bad guy, and save the girl. Bill Murray is beaten, but as he withdraws he mumbles to De Niro, "... the facilitator of all your dreams, pal." It's subtle, but the meaning is: it was all a setup by the Bill Murray character. I think people missed what an intelligent movie it was.

When Maria got back in Russia I sent her that movie. She understood what I was saying, of course. She is *so* clever.

I am not sure it took the sting off, though, but she has forgiven me for setting her up. If I understand correctly, in her 18 months in a windowless box she became something of a Christian. "Ballad of Reading Gaol," right?

Just to be clear, and since the Russian press reported it anyway, when she got out of her box and back to Moscow I sent her $1 million in Bitcoin. The Russian Communist Party (which hates her, she's their Ron Paul) made a fuss about it, acting like it means I control her. No, I did it thinking it was just the American Good Guy thing to do. Barr's DOJ had a snit about it with me but I let them know, "If there is one subject about which the USG can keep its opinions to itself with me, it is on the subject of my ethical duty to Maria Butina." I also got her to sign a piece of paper that she would never sue me or the DOJ for setting her up and putting her in a windowless box for 18 months, and DOJ was mollified by that.

That was generous. Still, for a man who admired Maria Butina, you misused her horribly.

Oh yes. I have noticed that it takes a while, but when people understand the whole story they see it from this angle. I am surprised it took you so long. Yes, absolutely, I make no pretense about it. I'm one of the several villains here. No doubt. She is wonderful gal and I misused her terribly in a scheme of my own. Guilty as charged.

Yes, you did. But…you respected and cared about Maria, clearly. "Deeply fond" of her, you said? You wanted to help her become President of Russia, right? Maybe you loved her but won't say. But you at least cared for her a lot. Right?

Yes.

Yet you fed her to the Deep State like a mouth guard into boiling water, to see what dental imprints the Deep State would make on her. Did I hear that correctly?

Yes.

Do you see anything contradictory there? Who does something like that?

[Byrne stares into the woods, perhaps thinking of the decades that separate him from his teenage self that ran these trails. Only after a long silence does Byrne answer.]

I suppose Arlen Specter didn't pick my name out of a hat.

It is the end of our last conversation with Byrne. After our long walk we have arrived back at our cars, and drive separate ways.

In the summer of 2022 Byrne testified to the J6 committee. Under oath, he confirmed the stories you have read here concerning setting up the Russian Collusion Hoax and a bribery-and-blackmail sting on Hillary Clinton, and setting up a rape-and-murder sting on Brennen, Comey and the Deep State.

See pages 202-203 and 255-257 of the transcript here https://rb.gy/oiqsl

FIGHT LIKE A ★★★ FLYNN

A PAC to Save America

"We have real enemies, dedicated to dominating and eventually destroying us, and they are not going to be talked out of their hatred".

"We will be unapologetic for standing up for American values and principles. America does not back down from anyone or anything."

TEXT: FLYNN 91776

"We are fundamentally responsible for securing the future of our people and we can pursue this goal boldly in the knowledge that doing so has the derivative effect of improving the lives of people around the globe."

Local Action results in National Impact but only if we make the decision to be courageous for our families, our communities and our country.
The time to stand up, step up and speak up is now.

Support us at: www.FightLikeAFlynnPAC.com

UNRAVELING THE RECESSION:

WHY AMERICA NEEDS A NEW COMMANDER-IN-CHIEF

By Mary Jones

The United States is facing a critical juncture as it grapples with the consequences of an ongoing recession. The economic downturn, exacerbated by the global pandemic, has left millions of Americans struggling with unemployment, rising inflation, and a growing wealth gap. As the nation searches for solutions, the pivotal role of leadership comes to the forefront. In 2024, America needs a new commander-in-chief who can navigate the complexities of the current economic landscape and steer the nation towards a path of recovery and prosperity.

Understanding the Economic Challenges:

Photo Source: CANVAPRO

To effectively address the recession, it is crucial to understand its underlying causes. The pandemic-induced shutdowns and subsequent supply chain disruptions caused widespread job losses and business closures, leading to a decline in consumer spending. The government's massive stimulus packages helped alleviate immediate hardships, but they also added to the national debt and raised concerns about long-term economic stability.

THE ROLE OF LEADERSHIP:

Photo Source: CANVAPRO

The upcoming 2024 presidential election provides an opportunity for the nation to elect a leader who can guide America through these trying times. A capable commander-in-chief can implement policies that support small businesses, stimulate job growth, and promote sustainable economic development.

Furthermore, effective leadership can foster confidence among investors, spur innovation, and encourage international trade, all of which are vital for a robust and resilient economy.

A VISION FOR RECOVERY:

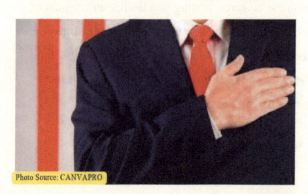

Photo Source: CANVAPRO

The next commander-in-chief must articulate a clear and comprehensive vision for economic recovery. This should include a focus on infrastructure investment, job creation, and targeted industry support. By prioritizing sustainable infrastructure projects, such as renewable energy development and modernized transportation networks, the new administration can create jobs while simultaneously addressing environmental challenges.

Moreover, an emphasis on retraining programs and affordable education can equip workers with the necessary skills to adapt to a rapidly evolving job market. By fostering a culture of innovation and entrepreneurship, the new leader can encourage the growth of industries that will drive future economic success.

ADDRESSING INCOME INEQUALITY:

Another critical aspect that the new commander-in-chief must tackle is the widening wealth gap. The recession has disproportionately affected low-income communities, exacerbating income inequality. Policies aimed at raising the minimum wage, improving access to affordable housing, and expanding healthcare coverage can help mitigate these disparities and promote social and economic equity.

In an interconnected global economy, the next president must prioritize international relations to ensure America's economic strength. Building and strengthening alliances, while also reengaging with international organizations, will foster cooperation on trade, investment, and technology.

By pursuing fair and mutually beneficial trade agreements, the new administration can open new markets for American businesses and promote economic stability on a global scale.

FOSTERING INTERNATIONAL RELATIONS:

Photo Source: CANVAPRO

Conclusion

As America faces the challenges of a recession, the importance of electing a new commander-in-chief in 2024 cannot be overstated. The next president must possess the vision, leadership skills, and policy acumen necessary to steer the nation towards a prosperous and inclusive future.

By focusing on economic recovery, addressing income inequality, fostering innovation, and strengthening international relations, the new administration can set the stage for a robust and resilient economy that benefits all Americans. The choices made in 2024 will shape the trajectory of the nation for years to come, making it imperative to select a leader who can unravel the recession and guide America towards a brighter future.

PROMOTING INDIVIDUAL LIBERTY:
BALANCING PERSONAL FREEDOMS AND GOVERNMENT INTERVENTION

By Andrew Joseph

In today's rapidly changing political landscape, one of the core debates centers around the delicate balance between personal freedoms and government intervention. As political conservatives and Christians, we value individual liberty and recognize the importance of limited government interference.

However, we also understand that certain situations call for responsible governance to safeguard the rights and well-being of all citizens. In this article, we explore the concept of promoting individual liberty while maintaining a careful equilibrium between personal freedoms and necessary government intervention.

Preserving Personal Freedoms

Individual liberty lies at the heart of the conservative ideology, emphasizing the belief that individuals should have the freedom to pursue their dreams, make personal choices, and enjoy the fruits of their labor. This principle recognizes that the government's primary role should be to protect these liberties rather than excessively regulate or dictate them.

For conservatives, preserving personal freedoms means advocating for limited government intervention in people's lives. It involves championing free-market capitalism, allowing individuals to participate in economic activities without undue government interference.

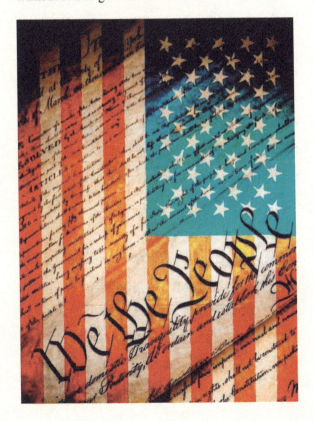

It also entails safeguarding civil liberties, such as freedom of speech, religion, and assembly, which are crucial for the expression of diverse opinions and ideas.

Balancing Personal Freedoms with Government Intervention

While personal freedoms are vital, it is equally important to acknowledge that there are situations where government intervention is necessary to ensure fairness, justice, and the overall well-being of society.

The challenge lies in striking a balance that upholds individual liberty while addressing societal concerns.

1- Safeguarding Public Safety and Security:
The government has a legitimate role in maintaining public safety and security. This includes measures such as law enforcement, national defense, and protection against external threats. Reasonable regulations and oversight are necessary to prevent criminal activities and maintain order, ensuring citizens can exercise their freedoms without fear.

2 - Promoting Social Equality:
While conservatives champion individual liberty, they also recognize the importance of providing

equal opportunities for all citizens. Government intervention can play a role in ensuring a level playing field by addressing systemic inequalities and removing barriers to advancement. For example, programs that promote education, job training, and entrepreneurship in disadvantaged communities can help individuals thrive and contribute to society.

3 - Safeguarding Moral Foundations:

As Christians, we believe in upholding moral values and principles that contribute to a healthy and flourishing society.

Government intervention can be justified when it protects the sanctity of life, defends traditional family structures, and preserves the fundamental

moral fabric of our communities. However, such intervention should be carefully balanced to avoid undue intrusion into personal beliefs and practices.

Conclusion:

Promoting individual liberty while balancing personal freedoms and government intervention is an ongoing challenge that requires thoughtful consideration and discernment. As political conservatives and Christians, we must navigate this complex terrain with wisdom, recognizing that while personal freedoms are crucial, responsible governance is also necessary to address societal concerns. By advocating for limited government interference, safeguarding civil liberties, and ensuring fair and just governance, we can maintain a society that upholds individual liberty while addressing the needs of all citizens. Striking the right balance allows us to create a society where personal freedoms flourish, where individuals can pursue their dreams, and where the principles we hold dear are upheld.

As we engage in this debate, let us approach it with a commitment to promote individual liberty, guided by the values and principles that have shaped our conservative and Christian traditions for generations.

DEFENDING NATIONAL SECURITY: PRIORITIZING A STRONG MILITARY AND SECURE BORDERS

By Johnson Hall

In today's complex and interconnected world, ensuring national security is of utmost importance. The protection of our citizens, the preservation of our values, and the safeguarding of our sovereignty depend on it. To effectively defend our nation, we must prioritize a strong military and secure borders. This article explores the vital role of these two pillars in maintaining national security.

A robust and capable military is the cornerstone of a secure nation. It serves as a deterrent against potential threats and ensures that we are prepared to defend ourselves when necessary. Investing in our military is not only about providing our armed forces with the necessary tools and resources; it is also about prioritizing the well-being of our servicemen and women. They are the brave individuals who voluntarily put their lives on the line to protect our freedoms and way of life.

Maintaining a strong military necessitates ongoing modernization efforts. Technological advancements, such as cyber warfare and unmanned systems, have transformed the nature of warfare. To stay ahead of emerging threats, we must allocate sufficient resources to research and development, ensuring that our military remains at the cutting edge of technology. Additionally, we must foster a culture of innovation and adaptability within our armed forces, equipping them with the necessary skills to navigate the evolving security landscape.

Secure borders are equally crucial in defending national security. Border control is not about xenophobia or isolationism; it is about ensuring that those who enter our country do so legally, while keeping out those who wish to harm us. By having effective border security measures in place, we can regulate the flow of people and goods, prevent human and drug trafficking, and identify potential security risks. Enhancing border security requires a comprehensive approach. This includes investing in physical barriers where appropriate, deploying advanced surveillance technologies, and bolstering the manpower of our border enforcement agencies. It also necessitates effective cooperation with international partners to address transnational threats and to share intelligence and best practices. By collaborating with other nations, we can create a united front against terrorism, organized crime, and other global challenges.

Critics argue that prioritizing a strong military and secure borders diverts resources from other important domestic issues. However, neglecting national security would be a grave mistake. Without a secure nation, all other priorities become secondary. It is the responsibility of the government to protect its citizens and uphold their rights, and this can only be achieved through a comprehensive approach that includes a strong military and secure borders.

Moreover, a secure nation fosters stability, which is essential for economic prosperity and individual freedom. When citizens feel safe, they are more likely to invest, innovate, and contribute to the growth of the nation. National security is not a hindrance to progress; it is a prerequisite for it.

In conclusion, defending national security requires prioritizing a strong military and secure borders. These two pillars are interconnected and indispensable in maintaining the safety, sovereignty, and values of our nation.

By investing in our military and implementing effective border control measures, we can protect our citizens, deter potential threats, and create an environment conducive to prosperity and freedom. As responsible citizens, let us recognize the significance of these priorities and advocate for their continued strengthening.

Photo Source: CANVAPRO

Made in the USA
Las Vegas, NV
18 September 2023